A YEARLONG WOMEN'S BIBLE STUDY GUIDE:

52 WEEKS OF DEVOTION, PRAYER AND SPIRITUAL GROWTH

Written by

Rev Minton Thomas

Thank You! Receive a Free Reflection Journal

Dear Reader,

Thank you for choosing *A Yearlong Women's Bible Study Guide.* It's my hope that this guide has been a blessing to you and brought you closer to God.

As a way to show my gratitude, I'd love to offer you a **Free Reflection Journal**! This companion journal, *Yearlong Bible Study Journal for Women: 52 Weeks of Scripture Prompts, Reflections, and Journaling,* is designed to help you deepen your spiritual journey through weekly prompts, reflections, and journaling space.

I would be grateful if you could take a moment to leave an honest review on Amazon for this book. Your feedback not only helps other readers find the book but also means the world to me.

To receive your **Free Reflection Journal**, simply leave a review and scan the QRcode below or follow this link below:

https://beacons.ai/revthomas

Thank you again for being part of this journey. I pray that this guide and the journal bring you closer to God every week.

Preface

In the quiet or busy moments between life's demands, many women find themselves searching for a deeper sense of purpose, faith, and identity. We navigate complex landscapes of expectation—family responsibilities, personal growth, and relationships—often feeling isolated in our spiritual journeys. This guide emerges from that sacred ground of vulnerability, recognizing that authentic femininity is forged not through external achievements, but through deep, intentional spiritual transformation.

Over the years, I've had the privilege of walking alongside women from diverse backgrounds, listening to their stories, and witnessing their hunger for a more authentic, meaningful faith. Women are seeking genuine connection—with God, with themselves, and with a faith that doesn't just inform, but fundamentally transforms. This 52-week journey is not a prescription, but an invitation. An invitation to strip away the masks of perfection, to confront internal struggles, and to rediscover femininity through Christ's radical example. Each week is carefully crafted to challenge, encourage, and ultimately reshape how you understand your spiritual identity.

Whether you're a seasoned believer seeking renewal or someone cautiously exploring faith's landscape, this guide meets you exactly where you are. It doesn't demand perfection but celebrates progress. It doesn't shame your struggles but illuminates pathways of grace. It doesn't complicate spiritual growth but simplifies the profound journey of authentic discipleship. My prayer is that these pages become more than words—that they become a mirror, a map, and a companion in your most intimate spiritual expedition. May each week mark not just knowledge gained, but character transformed.

Introduction

Welcome to a journey that spans millennia, a journey that transcends time and place to bring you into the presence of extraordinary women whose lives are woven into the very fabric of scripture. These women, whether renowned or seldom mentioned, have shaped the stories of faith, resilience, sacrifice, and wisdom that resonate deeply in our own lives today. "**A Yearlong Women's Bible Study Guide: 52 Weeks of Devotion, Prayer and Spiritual Growth**" is an invitation not only to learn about these women but to find yourself within their narratives, discovering how their lives echo into our own challenges, our own strengths, and our own walk with God.

Discovering a Rich Tapestry of Womanhood in Scripture

The women we meet in the Bible reflect the full complexity and beauty of what it means to be human. They are daughters, mothers, warriors, counselors, and prophets; they are women of courage and conviction, women who made mistakes and women who persevered through life's hardest moments. From women, who waited long years for their promise to come to fruition, to those who displayed remarkable wisdom and diplomacy in the face of conflict, to the Samaritan woman, who found freedom in the acceptance of Jesus—these women offer glimpses of the myriad ways God can use us in His unfolding story.

In this study, you will find stories of women who resisted oppression, built homes, stood up for justice, and leaned on God in moments of deep sorrow and overwhelming joy. Their lives reveal not only who they were but also who we can be. They provide us with examples to follow, wisdom to ponder, and warnings to heed, challenging us to examine our own lives and the role God calls us to play.

The Structure of Our Study

This study is designed to help you immerse yourself in each woman's story, guiding you through a four-part journey in every chapter. The structured approach allows you to build a meaningful connection with each woman, drawing both historical insights and personal reflections to enrich your faith.

- Meet:
Each chapter opens with an invitation to "meet" the character or theme for the week. Here, you'll delve into the context that shaped each woman's life—her background, culture, and circumstances. Whether she is standing up for her family, managing the trials of motherhood, or remaining faithful in obscurity, these introductions set the stage for a closer look at the nuances that make each woman's story both unique and universal.

- Lessons Learned:
What can we glean from the lives of these women? The Bible often shares only fragments of their stories, yet within these glimpses lies rich wisdom. In this section, we'll unpack their defining moments, choices, and relationships. What enabled Esther or the Samaritan Woman to act with courage when facing oppression? How did Deborah muster the bravery to act as a heroine in a time of national crisis? Through each life, we encounter timeless lessons that inspire and challenge us. Their experiences speak to our own fears, ambitions, and dilemmas, revealing how God's faithfulness and guidance can lead us through any situation.

- Finding Your Place:
In each week, after exploring the woman's story, we turn the lens inward to reflect on how these lessons apply to our own lives. Just as they encountered trials and moments of choice, so do we face decisions that shape our futures. This section provides space for reflection, asking thought-provoking

questions designed to help you discern how God is moving in your life. It's here that we explore questions like, "What does courage look like for me?" or "How can I cultivate wisdom in challenging relationships?" These moments of reflection help bridge the gap between ancient text and modern life, inviting you to engage with God's Word in a deeply personal way.

- Cultivating a Life of Prayer:
At the heart of each woman's story is a relationship with God, sometimes quiet and humble, other times bold and public. Prayer is both our response and our connection to God, grounding our lives and empowering us with His strength and purpose. In this final section, you'll find prayers inspired by each woman's journey—prayers that reflect the heart of the lesson and help you to seek God's presence in your own life. Whether you are asking for resilience, faith, or courage, these prayers serve as both guidance and invitation, encouraging you to embrace a life of intimacy with God.

Why This Journey Matters

Each chapter/week in this guide offers more than just historical knowledge; it invites you to walk alongside these women, to see the world through their eyes, and to experience God's work in their lives as it can be mirrored in your own. In their triumphs, you may find inspiration; in their struggles, you may find comfort; in their mistakes, you may find hope. As you journey through these stories, may you come to see that you, too, are a part of God's grand narrative, called to live a life of purpose, courage, and faith.

Whether you are a mother, a daughter, a friend, a leader, or simply a seeker, this study is crafted for you. The lessons embedded in each chapter are not just for reflection but for transformation, helping you to see how God can use your life, just as He used theirs. These women remind us that no matter

where we are, God is ready to meet us, guide us, and shape us
into vessels for His glory.

Preparing for the Journey

As you embark on this journey, come with an open heart and a
willingness to be challenged and changed. Let each story settle
into your spirit, allowing God's wisdom to speak to your heart.
Bring your questions, your hopes, your fears, and your dreams.
Use this time as a space to deepen your faith, strengthen your
character, and embrace the unique calling that God has placed
on your life.

In a world that constantly shifts, let these ancient stories ground
you in the unchanging truth of God's Word. May this study
guide serve as a beacon, a mentor, and a friend, leading you
toward a more profound relationship with the One who created
you, loves you, and calls you His own.

Let's begin this journey together, united by the legacy of these
faithful women and the timeless truth that God is faithful in
every generation.

Table of Contents

Week 1: Genesis - Eve, the First Woman

Meet: Eve, the Mother of All Living

Eve, the first woman created by God, is a pivotal figure whose story unfolds in the early chapters of Genesis. Formed from Adam's rib and brought to life by God's breath, Eve represents the beginning of womanhood and the establishment of the first human relationship. As the first woman, Eve's experiences in the Garden of Eden shape our understanding of human nature, the complexities of choice, and the impact of sin.

While often associated with the fall of humanity, Eve's story also reveals her strength, her capacity for love, and her role as a companion and also mother. Her journey through creation, temptation, disobedience, and ultimately, the promise of redemption, provides a rich tapestry of lessons for women navigating faith, relationships, and the challenges of life in a fallen world.

Lessons Learned

1. The Significance of Womanhood:

   - Genesis 1:27 states that God created man and woman in His image. It teaches women about their inherent dignity and value as God's creation, possessing intrinsic worth and potential.

2. The Power of Choice:

   - Eve's decision to eat the forbidden fruit (Genesis 3:6) demonstrates the reality of free will and the impact of choices on our lives and relationships, highlighting that we are responsible for the consequences of our decisions.

3. The Consequences of Disobedience:

   - Genesis 3:16-19 depicts the consequences of disobedience, highlighting the challenges and burdens that can follow sin, including pain in childbirth, a struggle for dominance in relationships, and the potential for conflict.

4. The Impact of Temptation:

   - The serpent's temptation (Genesis 3:1-5) reminds women of the power of temptation and the importance of discernment, recognizing the subtle ways in which sin can be presented as desirable.

5. The Power of Vulnerability:

   - Eve's vulnerability to the serpent's lies (Genesis 3:1-5) illustrates how important it is to be cautious about the influences that can lead us astray, reminding women to guard their hearts and minds.

6. The Strength of Love:

   - The love between Eve and Adam (Genesis 2:25) highlights the beauty and significance of human connection, reminding women of the power of love to bring joy and fulfillment, and the importance of nurturing healthy and fulfilling relationships.

7. The Role of Motherhood:

   - Eve's role as the mother of all living (Genesis 3:20) underscores the importance of motherhood and the profound influence women have on generations to come, reminding women that their choices and actions can have a lasting impact.

8. The Hope for Restoration:

   - Even after the fall, God expresses compassion and provides hope for restoration (Genesis 3:15), demonstrating His desire to redeem and restore relationships, offering women hope for a future of healing and redemption.

9. The Importance of Personal Identity:
   - Eve's creation as a partner and complement to Adam (Genesis 2:18-23) teaches women about the value of their unique identity, created in God's image and possessing inherent worth and significance.

Finding Your Place

Embrace your inherent dignity and value as a woman created in God's image. Trust in your God-given ability to make choices, recognizing the impact of your decisions on your life and those around you. Be mindful of the consequences of disobedience and seek to live in a way that honors God. Discern and resist temptation, protecting yourself from influences that lead astray. Embrace your vulnerability, recognizing that it does not diminish your strength or worth. Cherish the power of love in your relationships, allowing it to bring joy and fulfillment. Value and celebrate your role as a woman, understanding the impact you can have on the world around you. Hold onto the hope for restoration and renewal, believing in God's plan for redemption. Embrace your unique identity, understanding that God created you with purpose and intention.

Cultivating a Life of Prayer

Heavenly Father, Creator of all, thank You for the gift of womanhood and the beauty of Your creation. Help me to understand and embrace my identity as a woman made in Your image. Guide me in making wise choices, recognizing the impact of my decisions. Teach me to resist temptation and to protect myself from negative influences. Empower me to love deeply and to value the strength and significance of my role in the world. Remind me of Your plan for restoration and renewal, giving me hope for the future. May my life reflect Your love and grace. In Jesus' name, Amen.

Week 2: Exodus - Miriam, Sister of Moses

Meet: Miriam, the Prophetess and Leader

Miriam, the older sister of Moses and Aaron, emerges in the book of Exodus as a woman of strength, leadership, and prophetic gifting. Her courage and faith are evident from a young age as she watches over her baby brother Moses, placed in a basket among the reeds of the Nile River to escape Pharaoh's decree. As the Israelites journey through the wilderness, Miriam takes on a leadership role, often depicted as a prophetess and a songstress.

She leads the women in celebratory songs and dances after their miraculous deliverance at the Red Sea, expressing their gratitude and praising God for their freedom. However, Miriam's story also includes a challenging episode where she questions Moses' authority and faces the consequences of her actions. Through her journey, we witness the complexities of leadership, the importance of humility, and the unwavering faithfulness of God.

Lessons Learned

1. Courageous Protector:
   - Miriam's bravery in watching over baby Moses (Exodus 2:4-10) teaches women the importance of courageously protecting those who are vulnerable and standing up for what is right, even when facing powerful opposition.

2. Faithful Leadership:
   - Miriam's role as a prophetess and leader among the women (Exodus 15:20-21) highlights the significance of women in leadership positions within the community of faith, using their voices and gifts to guide and inspire others.

3. The Power of Praise:
   - Miriam's leading the women in song and dance after crossing the Red Sea (Exodus 15:20-21) emphasizes the transformative power of praise, expressing gratitude to God for His deliverance, and celebrating victories together.

4. The Dangers of Pride:
   - The incident where Miriam and Aaron challenge Moses' authority, questioning his marriage to a Cushite woman (Numbers 12:1-2), serves as a reminder about the dangers of pride and the importance of remaining humble before God, recognizing that true leadership comes from Him.

5. The Importance of Unity:
   - The conflict between Miriam, Aaron, and Moses (Numbers 12:1-15) illustrates the necessity of unity among leaders and the need to address disagreements with respect and humility, seeking reconciliation and understanding rather than division.

6. God's Faithfulness in Discipline:
   - Miriam's experience with leprosy, a consequence of challenging God's chosen leader, and her subsequent healing after Moses' intercession (Numbers 12:10-15) reminds women that even when we falter, God's discipline is rooted in love and leads to restoration when we humble ourselves and seek forgiveness.

7. The Gift of Prophecy:
   - Miriam's prophetic role, as evidenced when she receives divine messages and speaks God's words to the people (Exodus 15:20), encourages women to embrace their spiritual gifts and to use them to serve God and their community.

8. The Significance of Sisterhood:
   - Miriam's close relationship with her brothers, Moses and Aaron, offering support and encouragement throughout their

leadership journey, highlights the importance of supportive relationships and the strength found in sisterhood.

9. Leaving a Legacy of Faith:
   - Though not always perfect, Miriam's life leaves a legacy of faith and leadership, inspiring women to embrace their calling and to make a difference in the world.

Finding Your Place

Embrace your courage to protect the vulnerable and advocate for what is right. Step into your calling as a leader, using your voice and gifts to serve God and your community. Cultivate a heart of gratitude and express your praise to God through song, prayer, and joyful living. Guard against pride and strive for humility in all your interactions. Seek unity and understanding when disagreements arise, addressing conflict with respect and love. Remember that God's discipline is rooted in love and leads to restoration. Embrace the unique spiritual gifts God has given you, using them to bless others. Nurture supportive relationships with other women, finding strength and encouragement in sisterhood. Leave a legacy of faith that inspires others to follow God wholeheartedly.

Cultivating a Life of Prayer

Faithful God, who calls us to serve, may I be inspired by the example of servanthood. Strengthen my courage to protect those in need, and help me to lead with faith and humility. Fill my heart with gratitude and joy as I express my praise to You. Guide me in navigating disagreements with grace and understanding, seeking unity and reconciliation. May I embrace the gifts You have given me, using them to serve Your purposes. Surround me with a community of strong women who inspire and uplift me. Let my life reflect a legacy of faith and love that points others to You. In Jesus' name, Amen.

Week 3: Leviticus - Women and Ritual Purity

Meet: Women in the Mosaic Law

The book of Leviticus, a central part of the Torah, outlines the laws and rituals for the Israelites, including those pertaining to ritual purity. These laws, while often seen as complex and challenging, were intended to safeguard the people's health and spiritual well-being, and to maintain a distinction between the sacred and the profane. While women are not explicitly the focus of Leviticus, they are directly impacted by its laws and play a significant role in the practices of ritual purity.

The regulations surrounding childbirth, menstruation, and other aspects of women's lives offer a glimpse into the social and spiritual practices of the time. While these laws might seem restrictive or outdated from a modern perspective, understanding the context and meaning behind them can offer valuable insights into how women navigated faith, family, and social expectations in ancient Israel.

Lessons Learned

1. The Importance of Ritual Purity:
  - Leviticus 11-15 outlines various laws regarding ritual purity, including those related to food, hygiene, and bodily functions. This emphasizes the need for careful practices to maintain spiritual and physical well-being.

2. The Role of Women in Ritual Practices:
  - Women were responsible for observing and upholding specific ritual laws related to childbirth, menstruation, and other bodily functions (Leviticus 12, 15). It illustrates the active role women played in maintaining the spiritual purity of the community.

3. The Significance of Cleanliness:
   - The emphasis on cleanliness and purification in Leviticus highlights the importance of maintaining spiritual purity and holiness. This reminds women to seek a clean heart and a pure spirit in their relationship with God.

4. God's Compassion for Women:
   - The provision for women's periods and childbirth (Leviticus 12) reveals God's understanding of their unique biological needs and His desire to care for them.

5. The Impact of Rituals on Daily Life:
   - The integration of ritual laws into the daily life of the people underscores the importance of incorporating spiritual practices into everyday activities. It encourages women to seek God in every aspect of their lives.

6. The Concept of Consecration:
   - The laws surrounding the priest's purity (Leviticus 21) emphasize the concept of consecration, reminding women that they are called to live holy lives as reflections of God's holiness.

7. The Value of Community Support:
   - The communal nature of some rituals (Leviticus 12:6-8) highlights the importance of community support and shared responsibility in observing God's laws.

8. The Role of the Priesthood:
   - The role of priests in interpreting and enforcing the laws regarding purity (Leviticus 4-10) reminds women of the importance of spiritual leadership and guidance within the community.

9. The Promise of Restoration:
   - The overarching theme of atonement and purification within Leviticus points to God's desire for restoration and

reconciliation, reminding women that through God's grace, they can experience wholeness and redemption.

Finding Your Place

Embrace the importance of spiritual purity in your life, seeking to maintain a clean heart and a pure spirit before God. Recognize the significance of your role in observing God's laws and in upholding the spiritual purity of your community. Integrate spiritual practices into your daily life, seeking God in all that you do. Strive to live a holy life, reflecting God's holiness in your actions and relationships. Value the support of your community, knowing that you are not alone in your journey of faith. Seek out spiritual guidance and leadership from those who are called to teach and guide. Trust in God's plan for restoration and reconciliation, remembering that His grace is sufficient for your transformation.

Cultivating a Life of Prayer

Lord, You are the source of holiness and purification, inspire me to understand the importance of spiritual purity in my life and to live in a way that honors You. Guide me in observing Your laws and practices, seeking to maintain a pure heart and spirit. Empower me to live a holy life that reflects Your character. Strengthen my faith community, fostering support and shared responsibility. May I seek the guidance of spiritual leaders and find hope in Your promise of restoration and reconciliation. In Jesus' name, Amen.

Week 4: Numbers - The Daughters of Zelophehad

Meet: The Daughters of Zelophehad, Advocates for Justice

The story of the daughters of Zelophehad unfolds in the book of Numbers, presenting a compelling case for justice and equality. Zelophehad, a man from the tribe of Manasseh, dies without a son, leaving behind five daughters. In a society where inheritance was traditionally passed down through the male line, these women boldly step forward to plead for their rightful inheritance, challenging the existing laws and traditions.

Their appeal to Moses and the elders highlights the importance of recognizing and honoring the rights of women, even when they are confronted with limitations and societal expectations. Their courage to speak truth to power and to advocate for justice sets a powerful example for women throughout history, demonstrating the strength of faith in the face of adversity and the transformative power of challenging societal norms.

Lessons Learned

1. The Courage to Speak Up:
   - The daughters of Zelophehad bravely approach Moses (Numbers 27:1-4) with their request, demonstrating the importance of speaking up for what is right, even when it means challenging established norms.

2. Advocating for Justice:
   - Their plea for fair treatment (Numbers 27:3-4) emphasizes the necessity of advocating for justice, ensuring that everyone receives what is rightfully theirs.

3. The Importance of Equality:

- God's response to their request (Numbers 27:7-8) establishes a precedent for women's inheritance rights, highlighting the importance of equality and fairness in God's eyes.

4. Honoring God's Law:

- The daughters of Zelophehad appeal to Moses on the basis of God's law (Numbers 27:4). It reminds women to base their arguments and actions on God's Word and principles.

5. The Power of Persistence:

- The daughters' persistence in seeking justice (Numbers 27:1-11) shows the importance of persevering in the face of adversity and not giving up on their convictions.

6. The Role of Community in Change:

- The involvement of Moses and the elders in addressing their plea (Numbers 27:1-8) highlights the importance of community involvement in enacting positive change.

7. God's Justice and Fairness:

- God's response to their request (Numbers 27:7-8) demonstrates His desire for justice and fairness, even when it involves challenging existing traditions.

8. The Strength of Faith:

- The daughters' courage and determination are rooted in their faith in God. It encourages women to trust in God's power to bring about justice and change.

9. Leaving a Legacy of Justice:

- The daughters' actions leave a lasting impact on the law of inheritance, inspiring future generations to advocate for equality and justice.

Finding Your Place

Embrace the courage to speak up when you see injustice, advocating for fairness and equity. Remember that your voice matters and can impact change. Stand up for your rightful place and dignity, knowing you are worthy of being treated fairly. Base your arguments and actions on God's Word, seeking guidance and direction from His principles. Persevere in your efforts for justice, remaining steadfast in your convictions even when facing resistance. Engage with your community to advocate for positive change, working together to create a more just and equitable society. Trust in God's desire for justice and His power to bring about fairness for all. Allow your faith to empower you to challenge existing norms and to work for a better future. Be inspired by the daughters of Zelophehad, their legacy reminds us that women can be agents of change.

Cultivating a Life of Prayer

Righteous Judge, who hears and grants justice and equality, help me to recognize and fight against injustice in my life and community. Give me the courage to speak up for what is right and to stand firm in my convictions. Guide me to rely on Your Word as I strive for justice and equity. Grant me persistence and resilience in pursuing positive change, and may my actions inspire others to seek justice for all. May I always remember that You are a God of justice, and Your desire is for fairness and equality in the world. In Jesus' name, Amen.

Week 5: Deuteronomy - Women in Israelite Society

Meet: Women in the Mosaic Law

The book of Deuteronomy, meaning "second law" or "repetition of the law," presents a collection of Moses' final speeches and instructions to the Israelites as they prepare to enter the Promised Land. While not a specific focus on women, Deuteronomy provides insights into their roles, rights, and responsibilities within Israelite society, offering a glimpse into the unique laws and cultural norms that governed their lives.

Deuteronomy outlines laws related to marriage, inheritance, property rights, and social justice, highlighting both the privileges and limitations women faced in ancient Israel. It also emphasizes the importance of women's roles in education, family life, and religious practices.

Lessons Learned

1. The Importance of God's Law:
   - Deuteronomy 6:6-7 emphasizes the importance of teaching God's laws to children. This reminds women of the significance of spiritual instruction in shaping future generations.

2. The Value of Education:
   - Deuteronomy 31:11-13 instructs Moses to teach the Israelites God's laws. It highlights the importance of education for both men and women, ensuring that they understand God's commands.

3. Responsibilities in Family Life:
   - Deuteronomy 22:5-7 outlines specific responsibilities for women in relation to marriage, including dress, behavior, and

conduct. This underscores the importance of women's roles within family structures and societal expectations.

4. The Right to Inheritance:
- Deuteronomy 21:15-17 addresses inheritance rights, establishing the right for daughters to inherit property if there are no sons. This demonstrates that women possessed some legal rights and protections under the law.

5. Protection from Exploitation:
- Deuteronomy 22:28-29 outlines specific laws concerning rape and the protection of women from abuse. This highlights the importance of justice and care for vulnerable women.

6. The Importance of Purity:
- Deuteronomy 22:13-19 addresses laws regarding premarital purity, highlighting the value of chastity and the importance of maintaining sexual integrity.

7. The Call to Humility:
- Deuteronomy 21:10-14 describes laws surrounding the treatment of war captives, reminding women that God values compassion and humility in their interactions with others.

8. Participation in Religious Practices:
- Deuteronomy 12:12 emphasizes the importance of celebrating feasts and gatherings. This encourages women to participate in religious practices and to celebrate faith together.

9. The Impact of Faithfulness:
- Deuteronomy 30:19-20 emphasizes the importance of choosing life through obedience to God's laws. This reminds women that their choices and actions have a lasting impact on their spiritual and physical well-being.

Finding Your Place

Embrace your role in teaching future generations about God's Word, understanding its importance in shaping spiritual growth. Seek to understand and apply God's laws, allowing them to guide your choices and actions. Value your role within family structures and strive to live in accordance with God's principles for relationships and conduct. Advocate for justice and fairness for women, ensuring that their rights and protections are upheld. Embrace the value of purity, recognizing the importance of living in accordance with God's standards. Cultivate a spirit of humility and compassion in all your interactions. Participate actively in religious practices and celebrations, drawing strength and encouragement from your faith community. Commit to obedience to God's laws, knowing that your choices impact both your spiritual and physical life.

Cultivating a Life of Prayer

Faithful Covenant Keeper, who instructs and empowers, thank You for the wisdom and instruction contained in Your law. Help me to understand and apply Your teachings in my life, nurturing my own faith and guiding future generations. Empower me to embrace my role within my family and community, seeking to live in accordance with Your principles. Grant me courage to advocate for justice and to promote the dignity of women. Teach me to live a life of purity and humility, reflecting Your character. Strengthen my faith community and help me to celebrate Your presence in our lives. May my choices and actions always reflect my commitment to Your Word and Your will. In Jesus' name, Amen.

Week 6: Joshua - Rahab, the Faithful Harlot

Meet: Rahab, the Courageous Woman of Jericho

Rahab, a woman of Jericho whose story unfolds in the book of Joshua, embodies courage, faith, and redemption. Introduced as a harlot, Rahab's life takes a dramatic turn when she encounters two Israelite spies sent by Joshua to scout out the city. Recognizing the power of the God of Israel, Rahab chooses to hide the spies, defying her own people and risking her life to align herself with the Israelites and their God.

Rahab's faith is not just a passive belief; it motivates her to act courageously, leading to her protection during the destruction of Jericho and her inclusion in the lineage of Jesus Christ. Her story demonstrates that God's grace extends to all who seek Him, regardless of their past, offering a profound example of transformation and the unexpected ways in which God works through ordinary people.

Lessons Learned

1. Faith Beyond Fear:
   - Rahab's decision to hide the spies (Joshua 2:4-7) illustrates the power of faith to overcome fear, even when facing potential danger or social consequences.

2. The Courage to Be Different:
   - Rahab's willingness to defy her community and align with the Israelites (Joshua 2:9-11) demonstrates the courage to stand apart and embrace a different path based on conviction.

3. The Power of Hospitality:

   - By offering shelter and protection to the spies, Rahab exemplifies the importance of hospitality and extending kindness to strangers, recognizing the dignity of all people.

4. God's Mercy and Redemption:

   - Despite her past, Rahab's faith in God leads to her salvation and the preservation of her family (Joshua 6:25), showing that God's mercy and redemption are available to all who turn to Him.

5. The Significance of Actions:

   - Rahab's faith is not merely words but is demonstrated through her actions, highlighting the importance of aligning our beliefs with tangible expressions of faith.

6. Finding Strength in Vulnerability:

   - Although vulnerable as a woman in her society, Rahab displays remarkable strength and courage, reminding women that true strength can be found in faith and conviction, not social standing.

7. Stepping Out in Faith:

   - Rahab's act of tying the scarlet cord in her window (Joshua 2:18-21) symbolizes her bold step of faith, trusting in God's promise of protection and deliverance.

8. Transformation and New Beginnings:

   - Rahab's integration into the Israelite community (Joshua 6:25) emphasizes the possibility of transformation and new beginnings through faith in God.

9. Leaving a Legacy of Faith:

   - Rahab's inclusion in the lineage of Jesus (Matthew 1:5) shows that her act of faith resonated through generations, leaving a lasting impact on God's plan.

Finding Your Place

Embrace the courage to act on your faith, even when it requires you to stand apart from the crowd. Open your heart to those in need, extending hospitality and kindness regardless of their background. Trust in God's mercy and redemption, knowing that He welcomes everyone who seeks Him, regardless of their past. Allow your faith to guide your actions, demonstrating your beliefs through tangible expressions of love and service. Find strength in your vulnerability, realizing that true strength comes from a relationship with God. Be bold in taking steps of faith, trusting in God's promises for protection and guidance. Embrace the possibility of transformation and new beginnings in your life through faith. Remember that your actions can have a lasting impact, leaving a legacy of faith for future generations.

Cultivating a Life of Prayer

Gracious Redeemer, who welcomes and transforms and sees beyond our past, help me to act on my convictions, trusting in Your power to protect me. Open my heart to be a source of hospitality and kindness. Remind me that Your mercy and redemption are available to all who seek You. May my faith be more than words, guiding my actions and choices. Fill me with Your strength, especially when I feel vulnerable, and empower me to take bold steps of faith, trusting in Your promises. Guide me towards transformation and renewal, allowing me to experience a new beginning in You. Let my life reflect Your love and leave a lasting legacy of faith for those who come after me. In Jesus' name, Amen.

Week 7: Judges - Deborah, Prophetess and Judge

Meet: Deborah, the Woman of Courage and Wisdom

Deborah, a prophetess and judge in Israel, stands out as a powerful figure of leadership and faith in the book of Judges. She is recognized for her wisdom, her ability to discern God's will, and her unwavering commitment to justice. Deborah's story highlights the importance of women in leadership roles and the strength they possess in standing up for what is right.

Her story unfolds during a period of great turmoil and oppression in Israel, when the people are being threatened by Canaanite forces. Despite the challenges and the societal expectations of her time, Deborah emerges as a leader, offering guidance and direction to the people and even leading an army into battle against their enemies.

Lessons Learned

1. The Importance of Divine Guidance:
   - Deborah's reliance on God's guidance (Judges 4:4-5) illustrates the significance of seeking God's will and wisdom before making decisions, particularly in leadership roles.

2. Courageous Leadership:
   - Deborah's willingness to lead the Israelites against their enemies (Judges 4:6-7) demonstrates the courage needed to step into leadership roles, especially when facing significant challenges.

3. The Power of a Prophetic Voice:

   - Deborah's prophetic role (Judges 4:4) highlights the importance of women using their voices to speak truth and to guide others in accordance with God's will.

4. The Importance of Strategic Planning:

   - Deborah's strategic approach to leading the Israelite army (Judges 4:12-14) emphasizes the value of thoughtful planning and preparation in leadership.

5. The Role of Women in Warfare:

   - Deborah's leadership in the battle against Sisera (Judges 4) reminds women that they can be actively involved in defending righteousness and justice, even in traditionally male-dominated roles.

6. The Significance of Faithfulness:

   - Deborah's unwavering dedication to serving God and her people (Judges 5) underscores the importance of remaining faithful in one's calling, even when facing adversity.

7. The Power of Humility:

   - Deborah's humility in attributing her victories to God (Judges 5:31) illustrates the importance of acknowledging God as the source of strength and success.

8. The Importance of Unity:

   - Deborah's leadership unites the Israelites under a common purpose (Judges 4:10), highlighting the significance of fostering unity and collaboration within the community of faith.

9. Leaving a Legacy of Justice:

   - Deborah's story inspires women to leave a legacy of justice and righteousness, influencing future generations through their courageous actions and dedication to God's will.

Finding Your Place

Seek God's guidance in all your decisions, relying on His wisdom and direction. Embrace your calling to lead, using your skills and gifts to serve others and to make a difference. Use your voice to speak truth and to inspire those around you with the wisdom God has given you. Plan carefully, preparing for challenges and opportunities with strategic thinking. Remember that you can actively participate in defending righteousness, even in traditionally male-dominated spheres. Stay committed to your calling, persevering in your faith even when facing opposition. Cultivate humility, acknowledging God as the source of your strength and success. Foster unity and collaboration in your community, working together to achieve common goals. Leave a legacy of justice and faithfulness that inspires those who come after you.

Cultivating a Life of Prayer

Wise Counselor, who endows strength and wisdom, thank You for courage and wisdom and empowering us to lead,. Help me to seek Your guidance in my life and to embrace the calling You have placed upon me. Strengthen my courage to step into leadership roles, and empower me to use my voice to speak Your truth. Teach me to plan strategically and to act with wisdom and discernment. May I be a woman of faith, standing firm in my convictions and inspiring others to serve You with dedication. Guide me to foster unity and to leave a legacy of justice and righteousness. In Jesus' name, Amen.

Week 8: Ruth - Ruth's Loyalty and Faithfulness

Meet: Ruth, the Loyal and Faithful

The book of Ruth, set during the time of the judges, tells the story of a Moabite woman named Ruth whose loyalty and faithfulness play a pivotal role in the narrative. After the death of her husband and the subsequent return of her mother-in-law Naomi to Bethlehem, Ruth chooses to stay with Naomi rather than return to her own people.

Her commitment and devotion are evident as she supports Naomi and works diligently to provide for them both. Ruth's actions and decisions reflect a deep faith and trust in God's providence. Her story concludes with her marriage to Boaz, which not only ensures her future but also secures her place in the genealogy of King David and, ultimately, Jesus Christ. Ruth's faithfulness and loyalty are celebrated as exemplary virtues that contribute to her legacy and the unfolding of God's plan.

Lessons Learned

1. The Power of Loyalty:
   - Ruth's unwavering commitment to Naomi (Ruth 1:16-17) highlights the importance of loyalty in relationships. It teaches women to remain faithful to their loved ones, even when faced with challenges.

2. The Importance of Compassion:
   - Ruth's compassion for Naomi (Ruth 1:16-17) demonstrates that true compassion involves not just sympathy but also action and selflessness.

3. The Value of Hard Work:
- Ruth's diligence in gleaning in the fields (Ruth 2:17-18) demonstrates the importance of hard work and dedication, showcasing her determination to provide for herself and Naomi.

4. Trust in God's Providence:
- Ruth's faith in God's plan (Ruth 1:16-17) emphasizes the importance of trusting in God's provision and guidance, even when the future is uncertain.

5. The Impact of Kindness:
- Boaz's kind treatment of Ruth (Ruth 2:14) shows the power of kindness and compassion in influencing others. It teaches women to extend kindness, even to those who are different from them.

6. The Importance of Humility:
- Ruth's respectful approach to Boaz (Ruth 2:10-13) highlights the value of humility, demonstrating that true strength comes from recognizing God's sovereignty.

7. The Blessing of Faithfulness:
- Ruth's commitment to her faith and her devotion to Naomi lead to a significant blessing (Ruth 4:13-17). It reminds women that faithfulness to God can bring unexpected rewards.

8. The Power of Intercession:
- Naomi's prayer on Ruth's behalf (Ruth 4:13) shows the power of intercessory prayer, encouraging women to pray for one another and to seek God's intervention.

9. The Significance of Legacy:
- Ruth's inclusion in the genealogy of Jesus (Matthew 1:5) emphasizes the importance of leaving a legacy of faith that inspires future generations.

Finding Your Place

Be loyal and committed to your relationships, standing by loved ones through challenges and difficulties. Cultivate compassion, expressing love and care through actions. Embrace hard work and dedication, using your skills and talents to support yourself and those you care for. Trust in God's providence, believing in His plan and guidance even when the future seems uncertain. Extend kindness to those around you, even when they are different from you. Practice humility and respect, recognizing God's sovereignty and authority. Remain faithful to God's will, understanding that it can bring unexpected blessings. Pray for one another, seeking God's intervention and guidance. Live in a way that leaves a lasting legacy of faith and love, inspiring others to follow God's path.

Cultivating a Life of Prayer

Loving Provider, who nurtures loyalty and faithfulness, guide and inspire me to be a loyal friend and to demonstrate compassion in my relationships. Grant me the strength to work diligently and to trust in Your providence. Teach me to extend kindness to others, even when they are different from me. May I walk humbly before You, recognizing Your sovereignty, and find unexpected blessings in my faithfulness. Guide me to pray for others and to seek Your intervention in their lives. Help me to live a life that leaves a legacy of faith and love, inspiring future generations to follow You. In Jesus' name, Amen.

Week 9: 1 Samuel - Hannah's Prayer

Meet: Hannah, the Woman of Prayer

Hannah, the wife of Elkanah, is a significant figure in the book of 1 Samuel whose story resonates with women facing infertility, pain, and longing. She deeply desires to have a child but faces the anguish of barrenness, a condition that carries social stigma and personal heartache. Hannah's story highlights the power of persistent prayer, the faithfulness of God, and the importance of dedicating our children to His service.

Her heart-wrenching prayer at the tabernacle, pouring out her soul to God in a moment of deep despair, is a powerful testament to the intimacy and honesty we can have with God. Her story reminds women that God hears our prayers, sees our pain, and responds with compassion and faithfulness.

Lessons Learned

1. The Power of Persistent Prayer:
   - Hannah's relentless prayer at the tabernacle (1 Samuel 1:9-11) teaches women about the importance of pouring out their hearts to God, even in moments of profound sorrow and longing. She doesn't give up, even when her prayers seem unanswered, demonstrating the need for persistent faith.

2. The Importance of a Vow:
   - Hannah's vow to dedicate her child to the Lord (1 Samuel 1:11) demonstrates her commitment to fulfilling her promise to God if He grants her request. It highlights the significance of making vows to God and remaining faithful to those commitments.

3. Trusting God's Timing:

- While Hannah experiences years of barrenness (1 Samuel 1:2), she continues to trust in God's timing and His plan for her life. Her story reminds women that God's timing is perfect, even when it doesn't align with our own desires.

4. The Blessing of Motherhood:

- God blesses Hannah with a son, Samuel (1 Samuel 1:19-20). It celebrates the joy and fulfillment that motherhood can bring and acknowledges the deep desires of women who long for children.

5. The Importance of Dedication:

- Hannah's dedication of Samuel to God's service (1 Samuel 1:27-28) demonstrates the importance of placing our children under God's authority and raising them in faith.

6. The Significance of Thanksgiving:

- Hannah's song of thanksgiving (1 Samuel 2:1-10) expresses her deep gratitude to God for His faithfulness. It encourages women to acknowledge and celebrate God's blessings.

7. Finding Strength in Weakness:

- Hannah's initial weakness and despair are transformed into strength and joy through prayer (1 Samuel 1:18). This teaches that God can turn our weaknesses into opportunities for growth and transformation.

8. The Impact of Faith on Future Generations:

- Hannah's faithfulness in raising Samuel had a profound influence on his life and ministry. It highlights how a woman's faith and parenting can shape future generations.

9. God's Faithfulness to His Promises:

- The story of Hannah exemplifies God's faithfulness to His promises, reminding women that God hears their prayers and responds with compassion and love.

Finding Your Place

Persevere in prayer, even when you feel discouraged or unheard, knowing that God is attentive to your cries. Be honest and authentic in your communication with God, expressing your emotions and needs without reservation. Maintain your faith, even when facing challenges and uncertainty, trusting in God's timing and plan. Offer your life, talents, and gifts to God, recognizing that all you have belongs to Him. Express gratitude for His blessings, seeking ways to show your appreciation for His faithfulness. Build relationships within your faith community, seeking support and encouragement from fellow believers. Dedicate your life to raising your children in faith, understanding the profound impact of a mother's love and influence. Allow your prayers to shape your life and leave a lasting legacy of faith.

Cultivating a Life of Prayer

Listening God, who answers prayers with grace, You hear the cries of the brokenhearted. You are a God who understands our deepest desires. May I continue to bring my needs and longing before You, trusting in Your strength to answer in Your perfect time. Guide me to embrace thankfulness and to express my gratitude for Your blessings. Strengthen me to persevere in prayer, even when it seems I have no answers, and to find encouragement in my faith community. May I raise my children in faith, knowing that my love and devotion will shape their lives. Grant me the boldness to seek Your miracles and to trust in the lasting impact of my prayers. In Jesus' name, Amen.

Week 10: 2 Samuel - Bathsheba's Story

Meet: Bathsheba, the Woman of Courage and Faith

Bathsheba, a woman of beauty and strength, finds herself at the heart of one of the most complex and tragic narratives in the Old Testament. Her story unfolds in the book of 2 Samuel as she becomes entangled in King David's sin and ultimately becomes his wife. While Bathsheba is often portrayed as the object of David's lust and the catalyst for his downfall, her resilience, courage, and faith in the face of adversity shine brightly.

Bathsheba's story highlights the devastating consequences of sin and the complexities of navigating power and relationships. Despite facing the betrayal of her husband and the loss of her firstborn son, Bathsheba demonstrates her faith in God's power to heal and to restore. Her journey exemplifies the strength of women to persevere through heartbreak and to find solace in the midst of hardship.

Lessons Learned

1. The Importance of Integrity:

   - Bathsheba's initial refusal to succumb to David's advances (2 Samuel 11:2-4) demonstrates the importance of upholding moral standards, even when confronted with power or temptation.

2. Facing the Consequences of Sin:

   - Bathsheba's experience with the death of her firstborn son (2 Samuel 12:15-18) reveals the devastating consequences of sin and the pain it can bring.

3. The Power of Forgiveness:
- Despite being wronged, Bathsheba eventually forgives David (2 Samuel 11:27) and later becomes his wife, illustrating the transformative power of forgiveness and the grace that can heal broken relationships.

4. The Importance of Courage:
- Bathsheba confronts David about his actions (2 Samuel 12:13-14), demonstrating her strength and courage to speak truth to power, even when it is difficult.

5. The Role of Faith in Restoration:
- Bathsheba's faith in God's power to heal and restore (2 Samuel 12:16-25) reminds women that even after experiencing betrayal and hardship, God can provide renewal and hope.

6. The Significance of Motherhood:
- Bathsheba's experience as a mother, both the loss of her first son and the birth of Solomon, highlights the powerful role of motherhood and the challenges that women face in this role.

7. The Impact of Decisions:
- Bathsheba's story serves as a reminder that our choices have consequences, both for ourselves and for those around us, and the need to carefully consider the impact of our actions.

8. The Strength of Women:
- Bathsheba's journey through adversity and her eventual acceptance as queen (2 Samuel 12:24) demonstrates the strength and resilience of women in facing difficult circumstances.

9. The Hope of Redemption:
- While Bathsheba's story is marked by tragedy, it also points to the possibility of redemption and the ultimate triumph of God's grace.

Finding Your Place

Uphold moral integrity, even in the face of temptation or pressure, recognizing that your actions have consequences. Understand the devastating effects of sin and seek forgiveness and restoration when you falter. Find the courage to speak truth to power, even when it's difficult, and to advocate for what is right. Trust in God's power to heal and restore, even after experiencing betrayal and hardship. Embrace the challenges and joys of motherhood, cherishing the unique role you play in the lives of your children. Make wise choices, considering the impact of your decisions on yourself and others. Remember that you possess inner strength and resilience, capable of navigating difficult situations. Hold onto hope for redemption and the possibility of a renewed future through God's grace.

Cultivating a Life of Prayer

Forgiving Savior, who restores and redeems, teach me to understand the importance of integrity and to stand firm in my convictions, even when tempted. Guide me in seeking forgiveness and healing after I have made mistakes. Grant me the courage to speak truth, even when it is challenging. Strengthen my faith to trust in Your power to heal and restore, even after hardship. Give me wisdom to navigate the challenges of motherhood and to cherish the role You have given me. May I find strength in my faith and embrace hope for a renewed future through Your grace. In Jesus' name, Amen.

Week 11: 1 Kings - Wisdom of the Queen of Sheba

Meet: The Queen of Sheba, the Seeker of Wisdom

The Queen of Sheba, a powerful and wealthy monarch, is introduced in 1 Kings as a woman of great curiosity and discernment. Intrigued by reports of King Solomon's wisdom and the splendor of his kingdom, she embarks on a long journey to Jerusalem to see for herself. The Queen of Sheba's visit to Solomon is a testament to her desire for knowledge and her recognition of true wisdom.

Her encounter with Solomon, where they engage in thought-provoking discussions, challenges, and observations, exemplifies the importance of seeking wisdom and understanding. The Queen of Sheba's journey inspires women to pursue knowledge, to challenge their assumptions, and to recognize the value of godly leadership.

Lessons Learned

1. The Pursuit of Wisdom:

- The Queen of Sheba's journey to Jerusalem (1 Kings 10:1-2) demonstrates the value of actively seeking wisdom and knowledge, even when it requires effort and sacrifice.

2. Discernment and Observation:

- The Queen carefully observes Solomon's kingdom and engages in dialogue with him (1 Kings 10:4-9), highlighting the importance of using discernment and making astute observations when evaluating situations or leaders.

3. The Value of Questions:

- The Queen's thoughtful inquiries (1 Kings 10:3-4) emphasize the importance of asking questions to gain a deeper understanding and to challenge one's perspectives.

4. Recognizing True Leadership:

- The Queen's acknowledgment of Solomon's wisdom and the prosperity of his kingdom (1 Kings 10:6-7) teaches the value of recognizing and honoring those who possess godly leadership qualities.

5. Humility in the Face of Wisdom:

- The Queen's response to Solomon's wisdom, stating that "half of the greatness of your wisdom was not told to me" (1 Kings 10:7), demonstrates humility and a willingness to learn from others.

6. The Impact of Wisdom on a Nation:

- The Queen of Sheba's recognition of the prosperity and order in Solomon's kingdom (1 Kings 10:4-5) illustrates how wise leadership impacts the wellbeing of a nation.

7. The Generosity of Spirit:

- The exchange of gifts between the Queen and Solomon (1 Kings 10:10, 13) highlights the importance of generosity and mutual respect in relationships.

8. The Value of Cross-Cultural Exchange:

- The Queen's journey from a distant land to interact with Solomon encourages the value of cross-cultural exchanges for learning and building relationships.

9. The Pursuit of Excellence:

- The Queen's determination to witness Solomon's wisdom firsthand inspires women to strive for excellence in their lives and to seek out those who embody exceptional qualities.

Finding Your Place

Actively pursue knowledge and wisdom, recognizing its value in making informed decisions. Cultivate discernment and make thoughtful observations, allowing yourself to challenge your assumptions. Ask questions to gain a deeper understanding of the world around you and to expand your perspectives. Recognize and honor those who embody godly leadership qualities, seeking out mentorship and guidance. Practice humility when encountering wisdom, acknowledging that you can always learn from others. Be generous in your interactions, sharing your resources and knowledge with those around you. Engage in cross-cultural exchanges, learning from diverse perspectives and experiences. Strive for excellence in all areas of your life, seeking to emulate the virtues and strengths of others.

Cultivating a Life of Prayer

Source of Wisdom, who enlightens and guides, grants me understanding and discernment to courageously seek knowledge and wisdom. Help me to cultivate a thirst for knowledge, to ask thoughtful questions, and to learn from those who embody Your wisdom. Grant me discernment to recognize true leadership and to appreciate the impact of godly wisdom. Instill in me a spirit of humility, generosity, and a desire to strive for excellence in all that I do. May I be open to learning from diverse perspectives and experiences, embracing opportunities to expand my understanding of Your world. In Your name, I pray. Amen.

Week 12: 2 Kings - Widow's Oil Miracle

Meet: The Widow of Zarephath, a Woman of Faith

The story of the widow of Zarephath, as recounted in 2 Kings, is a testament to God's faithfulness and His provision in times of desperate need. Living in a land ravaged by famine, the widow faces the heart-wrenching prospect of losing her only son. Just as she is about to succumb to despair, she encounters the prophet Elijah, who brings a message of hope and a miraculous intervention.

This story highlights the power of faith in the face of hardship, the unexpected ways God works through His servants, and the importance of trusting in His provision. It encourages women to hold onto hope, even when circumstances seem bleak, and to believe in God's ability to work wonders.

Lessons Learned

1. The Power of Faith in Hardship:
   - The widow's initial act of hospitality to Elijah (2 Kings 4:8-10), despite her own desperate circumstances, illustrates the importance of faith in the face of hardship. It reminds women that even when facing poverty and loss, they can still find strength in trusting God.

2. The Importance of Obedience:
   - The widow's obedience to Elijah's instructions (2 Kings 4:10-11), though seemingly illogical, demonstrates her trust in God's guidance. This teaches women the value of listening to God's voice and acting according to His will, even when it seems difficult or illogical.

3. God's Provision in Times of Need:

- The miracle of the multiplying oil (2 Kings 4:14-16) highlights God's faithfulness in providing for those who trust in Him. It encourages women to believe that God willMeet their needs, even in desperate times.

4. The Strength in a Community of Faith:

- The widow's connection with Elijah (2 Kings 4:8-16) demonstrates the importance of seeking guidance and support from fellow believers. It reminds women of the strength found in a community of faith.

5. The Power of God's Servants:

- Elijah's role as God's instrument in working this miracle (2 Kings 4:14-16) reminds women that God works through ordinary people to bring about extraordinary things. It inspires women to trust in God's call and to seek ways to serve Him.

6. The Significance of Generosity:

- The widow's act of sharing her remaining oil (2 Kings 4:10-11) highlights the importance of generosity, even when resources are scarce. It encourages women to be willing to share what they have with others in need.

7. The Hope for a Renewed Future:

- The widow's experience of being rescued from poverty and despair (2 Kings 4:14-17) demonstrates the hope that exists for a renewed future, even after hardship. It reminds women that God can bring about transformation and restoration in their lives.

8. The Power of God's Word:

- Elijah's message to the widow (2 Kings 4:10) reminds women of the power of God's Word to bring hope and to guide their lives. It encourages women to study and to live according to God's Word.

9. The Importance of Trust:
   - The widow's trust in Elijah and God (2 Kings 4:8-16)
demonstrates the importance of trust in God's plan and in His
chosen servants. It teaches women to embrace faith and to
believe in God's promises.

Finding Your Place

Embrace faith as a source of strength in times of hardship,
remembering that God is faithful. Be obedient to God's will,
even when it seems challenging or illogical, trusting in His
wisdom and guidance. Believe that God will provide for your
needs, even in desperate times, and seek His provision. Build
strong relationships within your faith community, seeking
encouragement and support from fellow believers. Recognize
that God works through ordinary people to bring about
extraordinary things. Be generous in sharing your resources and
time with others in need. Hold onto hope for a renewed future,
trusting in God's power to transform your circumstances. Study
God's Word and allow it to guide your life. Embrace trust in
God's plan and in His chosen servants.

Cultivating a Life of Prayer

Miracle Worker, who provides abundantly, I pray for
unwavering faith. Inspire me to trust in Your provision, even
when my circumstances seem bleak. Guide me in embracing
obedience to Your will, even when it is difficult. Empower me
to be generous with my resources and to share with those in
need. Strengthen my faith community and help me to find
support and encouragement from fellow believers. May I be
open to God working through me to bring about Your purposes.
Remind me of Your faithfulness and Your power to bring about
transformation and renewal in my life. In Jesus' name, Amen.

Week 13: 1 Chronicles - Women in the Davidic Lineage

Meet: The Women of David's Ancestry

The book of 1 Chronicles chronicles the history of Israel, including the lineage of King David. While primarily focusing on the kings and their deeds, the text also highlights the significant roles of women in shaping David's lineage and influencing the history of the nation. These women, often overlooked in historical accounts, played a crucial role in perpetuating the covenant line that ultimately led to the birth of Jesus.

Despite facing social stigma, adversity, and complex circumstances, become integral threads in the tapestry of David's lineage and ultimately, the lineage of Jesus Christ. The inclusion of women in David's lineage underscores the importance of recognizing the contributions of women in shaping the course of history and the impact their choices and faith had on the unfolding of God's plan.

Lessons Learned

1. The Importance of Lineage:
   - 1 Chronicles 2:1-15 records the genealogy of Judah, emphasizing the importance of lineage and the way God uses families to fulfill His purposes. It reminds women that their role within their families is significant in God's plan.

2. The Power of Faithfulness:
   - The stories of women like Tamar (Genesis 38), Ruth (Ruth 1-4), and Abigail (1 Samuel 25) illustrate the power of faithfulness in difficult circumstances, demonstrating how women can be agents of change and protectors of their families.

3. The Impact of Choices:

   - The actions and choices of women like Tamar and Abigail (Genesis 38, 1 Samuel 25) show that women's decisions have a profound impact on the lives of their families and future generations.

4. God's Grace and Redemption:

   - The inclusion of women like Ruth, a Moabite, in the lineage of King David (Ruth 4:13-17) highlights God's grace and willingness to redeem and include those who are marginalized.

5. The Significance of Courage:

   - The boldness of women like Tamar (Genesis 38) in seeking justice and protection for themselves exemplifies the courage that women possess in standing up for what is right.

6. The Value of Wisdom:

   - Abigail's wise intervention in averting conflict (1 Samuel 25) highlights the importance of wisdom and discernment in navigating difficult situations. It reminds women of their God-given gifts for leadership and guidance.

7. The Role of Women in Spiritual History:

   - The inclusion of women in the lineage of David, who is considered a figure of great faith and influence, illustrates the significant role women play in spiritual history and the unfolding of God's plan.

8. The Strength of Family Ties:

   - The emphasis on lineage and family relationships emphasizes the importance of family connections and the enduring power of family bonds.

9. The Hope of a Future Messiah:

   - The lineage of David leads to the birth of Jesus Christ, the Messiah, highlighting the significance of lineage and God's plan for redemption through a descendant of David.

Finding Your Place

Recognize the importance of your role within your family and the impact your choices and actions have on future generations. Seek to live a life of faithfulness, even when facing difficult situations, trusting in God's power to guide and protect you. Embrace the lessons of courage and wisdom displayed by women in Scripture, seeking to act with boldness and discernment. Remember that God's grace extends to all, regardless of background or circumstances, and that you are included in His plan of redemption. Cherish the strength of family ties and invest in building strong and supportive relationships with your family members. Trust in God's ultimate plan for redemption and restoration, finding hope in the lineage of Jesus Christ.

Cultivating a Life of Prayer

Faithful Historian, who remembers and records, guide our generation to play significant roles in shaping history and the work of Jesus Christ. Help me to understand my importance within my family and the legacy I am building. Guide me to live a life of faithfulness, embracing courage and wisdom in my decisions. May I be a woman who reflects Your grace and extends mercy to those around me. Strengthen the bonds within my family, and may I find hope and strength in Your promises for the future. In Jesus' name, Amen.

Week 14: 2 Chronicles - Queen Mother Athaliah

Meet: Athaliah, The Queen of Idolatry

Athaliah, the daughter of King Ahab and Queen Jezebel, stands as a stark contrast to the righteous queens of Judah who came before her. She represents a period of great darkness in the history of Judah, marked by her relentless pursuit of idolatry and her ruthless attempt to seize power after the death of her son, King Ahaziah. Her story, as recounted in 2 Chronicles, highlights the dangers of unchecked ambition and the consequences of turning away from God.

Despite her power and influence, Athaliah's actions lead to a period of turmoil and bloodshed, ultimately resulting in her downfall. Her story serves as a cautionary tale for women, reminding them that the pursuit of power and self-interest can lead to destruction and that true leadership is rooted in serving God and His people.

Lessons Learned

1. The Dangers of Unchecked Ambition:
   - Athaliah's relentless pursuit of power (2 Chronicles 22:10-12) reveals the destructive nature of unchecked ambition, reminding women to prioritize righteousness and humility over personal gain.

2. The Consequences of Idolatry:
   - Athaliah's relentless pursuit of Baal worship (2 Chronicles 22:10-12) highlights the dangers of turning away from God and embracing false idols, demonstrating the importance of staying faithful to God alone.

3. The Importance of Spiritual Leadership:
   - Athaliah's attempt to eliminate the royal line (2 Chronicles 22:10-11) underscores the importance of spiritual leadership in protecting and guiding a nation, emphasizing the need for leaders who are dedicated to righteousness and justice.

4. God's Power to Restore:
   - The miraculous escape of Joash and his eventual coronation as king (2 Chronicles 22:11-23:1) demonstrates God's power to restore and to bring about His plan, even in the midst of turmoil.

5. The Role of the Priesthood:
   - The key role of the priest Jehoiada (2 Chronicles 22:11-23) in protecting the rightful heir and restoring the worship of God highlights the significance of spiritual guidance in times of crisis.

6. The Strength of Faithfulness:
   - The priest Jehoiada's unwavering commitment to God and his courage to confront Athaliah (2 Chronicles 23:1-15) illustrate the power of faithfulness in the face of adversity.

7. The Importance of Community:
   - The collective effort of the priests and the people in overthrowing Athaliah (2 Chronicles 23:1-15) emphasizes the importance of unity and collective action in upholding righteousness and protecting God's work.

8. The Need for Humility:
   - Athaliah's downfall (2 Chronicles 24:7) serves as a reminder of the importance of humility and the dangers of pride, showcasing the consequences of seeking power over serving God.

9. The Lasting Impact of Choices:
   - Athaliah's reign of idolatry left a lasting impact on Judah, teaching women to consider the long-term consequences of their actions.

Finding Your Place

Guard against unchecked ambition, prioritizing righteousness and humility over personal gain. Remain faithful to God alone, rejecting false idols and ideologies that can lead you astray. Seek to be a leader who upholds God's principles, guiding and protecting those around you. Trust in God's power to restore and to bring about His plan, even in challenging circumstances. Value the role of spiritual leaders in guiding and protecting communities. Maintain faithfulness to God, even in the face of adversity, and be willing to stand up for what is right. Embrace the importance of community, working together to uphold righteousness and to combat injustice. Cultivate humility and avoid pride, remembering that true leadership is rooted in serving God and others. Make choices with a long-term perspective, understanding the impact of your actions on your legacy and on those around you.

Cultivating a Life of Prayer

Sovereign Lord, who oversees justice and righteousness, reign over all creation for eternity. Guard us my God against the dangers of unchecked ambition, choosing humility and righteousness in my life. Guide me to be a faithful follower of Your ways, rejecting false idols and ideologies. May I seek to be a leader who upholds Your principles and who protects those around me. Strengthen my faith to remain steadfast in challenging times, trusting in Your power to restore and to bring about Your plan. May I be a part of a community that upholds Your truth and that strives for justice and righteousness. In Your name, I pray. Amen.

Week 15: Ezra - Foreign Wives: Navigating Cultural Identity and Faith

Meet: Foreign Wives, a Challenge to Faithfulness

The book of Ezra, set during the time of the return of the Israelites from exile in Babylon, highlights a significant challenge faced by the community: the integration of foreign wives into the Jewish faith. This cultural blending, while reflecting the changing landscape of the post-exilic era, also posed a threat to the spiritual purity and identity of the newly formed community.

Ezra, a dedicated scribe and priest, arrives in Jerusalem with a passionate commitment to God's Law, recognizing the need for a spiritual restoration. As he witnesses the intermarriage between Jewish men and foreign women, he confronts the community with a powerful call to repentance and separation, challenging them to return to the purity of their faith and to uphold the covenant with God. This confrontation raises critical questions about navigating cultural identity, maintaining spiritual integrity, and the role of leadership in guiding a community through times of transition.

Lessons Learned

1. The Importance of God's Law:
   - Ezra 7:6 emphasizes Ezra's commitment to studying and obeying the Law. It reminds women that God's Word should be the foundation of our lives and choices.

2. The Challenge of Cultural Blending:
   - Ezra 9-10 reveals the challenges of balancing cultural identity and faithfulness to God. It teaches women to navigate

complex situations with wisdom and discernment, seeking to remain faithful to God's principles even amidst cultural shifts.

3. The Need for Spiritual Purity:
   - The concern about intermarriage (Ezra 9-10) underscores the importance of spiritual purity, particularly when seeking to uphold God's standards in a changing world.

4. The Power of Repentance:
   - The community's response to Ezra's challenge, including confession and repentance (Ezra 10:6-11), illustrates the importance of acknowledging sin and seeking forgiveness.

5. The Role of Leadership:
   - Ezra's leadership in addressing the issue of intermarriage demonstrates the importance of leaders who champion God's Word and guide communities towards spiritual renewal.

6. The Significance of Unity:
   - The gathering of the people and their collective commitment to separating from foreign wives (Ezra 10:1-4) emphasizes the value of unity and collective action in upholding spiritual values.

7. The Call for Courage:
   - Ezra's courageous confrontation of the community (Ezra 9:1-15) shows the need to stand up for God's standards, even when it's difficult or controversial.

8. The Importance of Discernment:
   - Ezra's discernment in recognizing the threat of cultural assimilation (Ezra 9:1-2) reminds women to critically evaluate their surroundings and choices.

9. The Hope for Renewal:
   - Ezra's efforts to restore the people to faithfulness (Ezra 10:1-11) offer hope for spiritual renewal and restoration, even after periods of compromise.

Finding Your Place

Embrace God's Word as the foundation of your life, seeking to understand and live according to its teachings. Navigate cultural shifts and blending with wisdom and discernment, remaining faithful to God's principles. Prioritize spiritual purity, striving to live a life that honors God's standards. Acknowledge sin and seek forgiveness through repentance, allowing God's grace to restore you. Support leaders who champion God's Word and encourage spiritual renewal. Embrace unity with fellow believers, working together to uphold God's values. Be courageous in upholding God's standards, even when it's challenging. Exercise discernment in your life choices and relationships, ensuring that you remain grounded in God's truth. Hold onto hope for spiritual renewal and restoration, believing in God's ability to transform and restore your life and community.

Cultivating a Life of Prayer

Divine Protector, who ensures deliverance in times of need, I want to devote my life to Your people and to Your ways. Help me to understand and live by Your Word, grounding my life in Your truths. Grant me wisdom to navigate cultural complexities and to maintain my faithfulness in a changing world. Guide me in seeking spiritual purity and to embrace repentance when I fall short. Empower me to support spiritual leaders who champion Your Word and to foster unity within my community. May I be courageous in defending Your standards, discerning between truth and error, and seeking renewal and restoration. In Jesus' name, Amen.

Week 16: Nehemiah - Women in Rebuilt Jerusalem

Meet: The Women of Jerusalem, Rebuilding Lives and Faith

The book of Nehemiah recounts the story of Nehemiah, the cupbearer to King Artaxerxes, who is granted permission to return to Jerusalem and rebuild its broken walls. While the focus of the narrative is on the physical reconstruction of the city, the book also provides glimpses into the lives of women who contributed to the rebuilding efforts and the spiritual renewal of the community.

These women, though not always named or mentioned explicitly, played vital roles in supporting their families, participating in the work of rebuilding, and contributing to the spiritual rededication of Jerusalem. Their presence and actions highlight the importance of women in community building, the strength they possess in times of adversity, and their unwavering commitment to faith and restoration.

Lessons Learned

1. The Strength of Women in Rebuilding:

   - The women of Jerusalem, alongside the men, participated in the rebuilding of the city walls (Nehemiah 3:12), demonstrating their strength and resilience in contributing to the community's restoration.

2. The Value of Teamwork and Unity:

   - The collective effort of men and women in rebuilding the walls (Nehemiah 3) emphasizes the importance of teamwork and unity in achieving common goals.

3. The Importance of Family and Community:

- Nehemiah's concern for the welfare of the people (Nehemiah 5:1-13) highlights the significance of family and community support, recognizing the interconnectedness of individuals within the community.

4. The Power of Prayer:

- Nehemiah's consistent prayer throughout the rebuilding process (Nehemiah 1:4-11, 2:4, 4:4-5, 9) emphasizes the importance of prayer in seeking God's guidance and protection during challenging times.

5. Standing Firm in Faith:

- The community's determination to rebuild despite opposition and threats (Nehemiah 4) illustrates the strength of standing firm in faith, even when facing adversity.

6. The Joy of Celebration:

- The dedication of the wall (Nehemiah 12:27-43), involving both men and women, highlights the importance of celebrating victories and acknowledging God's faithfulness.

7. Commitment to Spiritual Renewal:

- The reading of the Law and the renewal of the covenant (Nehemiah 8-10) demonstrate the community's commitment to spiritual growth and renewal alongside the physical rebuilding.

8. The Role of Women in Worship:

- The presence of women in the dedication ceremony (Nehemiah 12:43) emphasizes the importance of women's participation in worship and religious celebrations.

9. The Legacy of Restoration:

- The efforts of the women in rebuilding Jerusalem contribute to a legacy of restoration, reminding women that their actions can have a lasting impact on their communities and future generations.

Finding Your Place

Recognize the strength you possess to contribute to the rebuilding and restoration of your community. Embrace teamwork and unity, working alongside others to achieve common goals. Value the importance of family and community support, recognizing the interconnectedness of individuals. Turn to prayer as a source of strength and guidance, seeking God's wisdom and protection. Stand firm in your faith, even when facing challenges, knowing that God is with you. Celebrate victories and acknowledge God's faithfulness in your life and community. Commit to spiritual renewal and growth, seeking opportunities to deepen your faith. Actively participate in worship and religious gatherings, finding strength and encouragement in your faith community. Leave a legacy of restoration, understanding that your actions can positively impact future generations.

Cultivating a Life of Prayer

Strengthening God, who raises up supporters for Your work, use me to rebuild broken walls and mend broken hearts as well even in my life. May I be inspired by their strength and resilience. Help me to embrace teamwork and unity, valuing the support of my community. Guide me in prayer, seeking Your wisdom and protection in challenging times. Strengthen my resolve to stand firm in my faith and to celebrate Your faithfulness. Empower me to be a part of Your work of restoration, leaving a legacy of hope and renewal for those who come after me. In Jesus' name, Amen.

Week 17: Esther - Esther, A Woman of Courage

Meet: Esther, The Queen Who Stood Up

Esther, a young Jewish woman living in the Persian Empire, is a powerful testament to courage and faith. Orphaned as a child, she is raised by her cousin Mordecai, who instills in her a deep sense of loyalty and faith. She is unexpectedly thrust into a position of power when she becomes the queen of Persia, a choice that brings both privilege and peril. Her story unfolds against the backdrop of a plot to exterminate the Jewish people, orchestrated by the wicked advisor Haman. This is where Esther's courage truly shines. Her story is a powerful example of how God can use unexpected individuals to bring about His purposes.

Esther's journey from a young woman in a foreign palace to a courageous advocate for her people illustrates the importance of standing up for what is right and using one's position for the greater good. Her willingness to risk her life to approach the king and reveal her identity showcases her strength and serves as a powerful reminder of the impact one person can have when they embrace their voice and purpose.

Lessons Learned

1. The Importance of Identity:
   - Esther's decision to remain silent about her Jewish heritage (Esther 2:10) highlights the importance of understanding and embracing one's identity, even in a challenging environment.

2. The Courage to Speak Up:
   - Esther's bravery in revealing her identity to King Xerxes (Esther 4:16-17) demonstrates the courage needed to stand up for what is right, even when facing significant risk.

3. The Power of Influence:
   - Esther's influence on the king and her ability to change the decree (Esther 8:3-8) underscores the importance of using one's position to make a difference.

4. The Strength of Prayer and Fasting:
   - Esther's call for the Jewish people to fast and pray (Esther 4:16) highlights the power of prayer and the importance of seeking God's intervention in times of crisis.

5. The Call for Justice:
   - Esther's stand against Haman's plot (Esther 7:3-4) demonstrates the need to stand up for justice, even when it means confronting evil.

6. The Importance of Faithfulness:
   - Esther's faithfulness to her people and to God (Esther 4:13-14) teaches women to be committed to their faith and to advocate for those who are vulnerable.

7. The Role of God's Providence:
   - The story of Esther highlights the idea of divine providence, suggesting that God works through unexpected circumstances to achieve His purposes.

8. The Power of a Single Voice:
   - Esther's courage to speak truth to power, even when facing great danger, shows that one voice can make a difference in standing against injustice and advocating for what is right.

9. Remembering God's Deliverance:
   - The establishment of the festival of Purim (Esther 9:20-22) highlights the importance of celebrating God's deliverance and remembering His faithfulness.

Finding Your Place

Embrace your identity and embrace the strength that comes from understanding your unique place in God's plan. Cultivate courage to speak up for what is right, even when it means facing fear or resistance. Recognize your influence and use your voice to make a difference in the world. Seek God's guidance through prayer, recognizing its power to bring about change and to sustain you in difficult times. Advocate for justice, defending those who are vulnerable and working to overcome oppression. Remain faithful to your convictions, standing firm in your beliefs. Trust in God's providence, believing that He works through even the most unexpected circumstances to accomplish His purposes. Remember that your voice, no matter how small, can have a significant impact. Celebrate God's faithfulness and deliverance, sharing your stories of hope with others.

Cultivating a Life of Prayer

Courageous King, who empowers bravery in adversity, use me to give courage to the fainthearted. Help me to embrace my unique identity in You and to use my voice to speak truth and to advocate for justice. Fill me with courage to face challenges boldly, trusting in Your plans and guidance. Strengthen my faith to stand firm against oppression and to celebrate Your faithfulness. May I find strength in my community, working together to bring about positive change. May my life be a testament to Your power and grace, inspiring others to live with courage and purpose. In Jesus' name, Amen.

Week 18: Job - Job's Daughters: Inheritance and Equality

Meet: Job's Daughters, Symbols of Restoration and Blessing

The book of Job, a profound exploration of suffering, faith, and the restoration of God's blessings, often focuses on the trials and tribulations of Job himself. However, amidst the narrative of loss and questioning, the story of Job's daughters emerges as a powerful testament to God's grace and His commitment to restoring what has been broken.

After Job endures unimaginable suffering, losing his wealth, his health, and even his children, God blesses him with a new family, including seven sons and three daughters. These daughters, specifically named—Jemimah, Keziah, and Keren-Happuch—are described as the most beautiful women in the land, and, remarkably, they receive an inheritance alongside their brothers. This act of inclusion and equality stands out in a patriarchal society, highlighting God's heart for fairness and the value He places on women.

Lessons Learned

1. God's Restoration Extends to All:
   - The restoration of Job's family, including his daughters (Job 42:13-15), highlights that God's blessings are not limited to material possessions but encompass the restoration of relationships and family.

2. The Value of Women:
   - The description of Job's daughters as the most beautiful women in the land (Job 42:15) emphasizes the inherent worth and beauty of women, challenging societal norms that often devalue women.

3. Inheritance Rights for Daughters:
   - The granting of inheritance to Job's daughters (Job 42:15) stands out in a patriarchal context, demonstrating that God values equality and fairness in the distribution of blessings.

4. The Significance of Names:
   - Each of Job's daughters is given a unique name (Jemimah, Keziah, and Keren-Happuch), suggesting that they are individuals with distinct identities and worth.

5. Beauty as a Reflection of God's Grace:
   - The beauty of Job's daughters can be seen as a reflection of God's grace and restorative power, highlighting how God can bring beauty from ashes.

6. Hope Amidst Suffering:
   - The birth of Job's daughters after his period of intense suffering (Job 42:10-17) offers a message of hope and renewal, showing that God can bring new life and joy even after loss.

7. The Importance of Family:
   - The restoration of Job's family underscores the importance of family ties and the blessings of having children.

8. The Power of God's Blessing:
   - The prosperity and recognition bestowed upon Job's daughters (Job 42:15) demonstrate the transformative power of God's blessings in one's life.

9. The Legacy of Faithfulness:
   - Job's faithfulness through suffering is rewarded with the blessing of a new family, including daughters who are honored and valued. This reminds women that God sees their faithfulness and will reward them in His time.

Finding Your Place

Trust in God's power to restore and bring beauty from ashes, even in the midst of loss and pain. Recognize your inherent worth and value as a woman, created in God's image and deserving of respect and honor. Advocate for equality and fairness, knowing that God values justice for all. Embrace the uniqueness of your identity and the gifts God has given you. Find hope in God's promises, believing that He can bring renewal and joy even after difficult seasons. Cherish the blessings of family and relationships, nurturing those connections. Trust in God's power to bless your life, recognizing His hand in your circumstances. Live a life of faithfulness, knowing that God sees your actions and will reward your commitment to Him.

Cultivating a Life of Prayer

Sustainer of Faith, who supports especially through trials, teach me to trust in Your power to heal and bring beauty into my life, even after times of suffering. Remind me of my inherent worth as Your daughter, worthy of respect and love. Guide me to advocate for justice and equality, reflecting Your heart for fairness. May I embrace the unique identity and gifts You have given me, and find hope and joy in Your promises. Bless my family and relationships, and help me to live a life of faithfulness, trusting in Your blessings and provision. In Jesus' name, Amen.

Week 19: Psalms - A Woman of Praise and Worship

Meet: The Women of the Psalms, Voices of Honesty and Devotion

The book of Psalms, a collection of prayers, poems, and songs, offers a diverse tapestry of human emotions and experiences in relationship with God. While many Psalms are attributed to King David, the book also includes contributions from other writers, including women. These women, though often unnamed, contribute their voices to the tapestry of human expression, offering insights into the unique challenges and joys of faith from a feminine perspective.

The Psalms provide a framework for women to engage in authentic worship, pouring out their hearts to God in times of joy, sorrow, doubt, and praise. They teach the importance of honesty in prayer, the power of expressing emotions, and the solace found in God's presence. These ancient words resonate across generations, providing timeless guidance for women seeking a deeper connection with God.

Lessons Learned

1. Honesty in Prayer:
   - The Psalms model raw and honest communication with God (Psalm 13, 61). They teach women to express their true feelings, anxieties, and doubts without reservation, knowing that God welcomes authenticity.

2. Finding Comfort in God's Presence:
   - Psalms like Psalm 23 and 46 offer a sense of peace and security in God's presence. They encourage women to seek refuge in their relationship with God, finding comfort and solace in times of trouble.

3. The Power of Praise:

- Many Psalms are filled with exuberant praise, acknowledging God's goodness and power (Psalm 100, 145). They teach the importance of celebrating God's faithfulness and expressing gratitude for His blessings.

4. Seeking Forgiveness and Repentance:

- Penitential Psalms, such as Psalm 51, provide examples of acknowledging wrongdoing and seeking God's forgiveness. It encourages women to approach God with humility, seeking restoration and renewal.

5. Trusting God through Trials:

- Psalms of lament, like Psalm 42 and 88, express struggles and hardships, while still holding onto faith in God. They teach women to trust in God's presence and faithfulness even when facing difficult times.

6. Reflecting on God's Creation:

- Psalms like Psalm 8 and 19 celebrate the beauty and wonder of God's creation. They encourage women to appreciate the natural world as a reflection of God's power and creativity.

7. The Importance of God's Word:

- Psalm 119 celebrates the power and beauty of Scripture. It challenges women to engage with God's Word, finding guidance and wisdom for their lives.

8. Expressing Gratitude:

- Many Psalms focus on expressing gratitude for God's faithfulness and provision (Psalm 107, 136). They encourage women to cultivate a thankful heart, acknowledging God's blessings in their lives.

9. Finding Strength in God:

- Psalms of confidence (Psalm 27, 121) demonstrate the strength and security that come from trusting in God. They inspire women to rely on God's power and presence in their struggles.

Finding Your Place

Engage with the Psalms as a guide for your own expressions of prayer and worship, using them to connect with God on a personal level. Be honest and authentic in your prayers, pouring out your heart to God in all your emotions. Seek comfort and refuge in God's presence, trusting in His love and care for you. Cultivate a lifestyle of praise and gratitude, celebrating God's goodness and expressing thanks for His blessings. Acknowledge your need for forgiveness and embrace repentance, allowing God to restore and renew you. Trust in God's faithfulness during trials, knowing that He is with you in every season. Reflect on the wonders of God's creation, finding inspiration and awe in the world around you. Engage with God's Word regularly, allowing it to guide and shape your life. Practice gratitude, recognizing God's hand in your everyday experiences. Find strength and courage in your relationship with God, relying on His power and presence to overcome challenges.

Cultivating a Life of Prayer

Worthy God, who receives our praise and worship, You listen to the whispers and cries of my soul. May my prayers be as authentic and heartfelt as those expressed in the Psalms. Guide me to find comfort in Your presence, to praise Your name with joy and gratitude, and to seek Your forgiveness when I stumble. Help me to navigate life's challenges with a heart of trust, celebrating the beauty of Your creation and drawing strength from Your Word. In Jesus' name, Amen.

Week 20: Proverbs - The Ideal Woman in Proverbs 31

Meet: The Woman of Noble Character

The book of Proverbs, filled with wisdom sayings and practical advice for daily living, culminates with a powerful description of an ideal woman in Proverbs 31:10-31. This passage, often referred to as the "Eshet Chayil" or "Woman of Valor," paints a vivid portrait of a woman of strength, wisdom, compassion, and industriousness.

This woman is not presented as a flawless individual but rather as one who embraces her various roles with diligence, skill, and a deep sense of purpose. Her qualities encompass both practical skills and spiritual virtues, highlighting the multifaceted nature of a godly woman. The "Woman of Valor" serves as an inspiring example for women of all ages, encouraging them to cultivate a life of purpose, strength, and faithfulness.

Lessons Learned

1. The Value of Hard Work and Resourcefulness:
   - Proverbs 31:13-19, 24-25 describe the woman's diligence in managing her household and her skillful use of resources. This teaches women the importance of hard work and being resourceful, using their talents to provide for their families and communities.

2. The Importance of Wisdom and Kindness:
   Proverbs 31:26 emphasizes the woman's wisdom and kindness in her speech and interactions. It reminds women to use their words to build up and encourage others, speaking with wisdom and grace.

3. The Strength of a Godly Woman:

- The description of the woman's strength and dignity (Proverbs 31:25) highlights the power of a woman who lives according to God's principles. It encourages women to embrace their strength and to use it for good.

4. The Value of Compassion and Generosity:

- Proverbs 31:20 depicts the woman extending her hand to the poor and needy. It emphasizes the importance of compassion and generosity, actively caring for those who are less fortunate.

5. The Importance of Planning and Preparation:

- The woman's foresight in preparing for her family's needs (Proverbs 31:15, 21) teaches women the value of planning and preparation in managing their households and responsibilities.

6. The Blessing of a Godly Home:

- Proverbs 31:28-31 describes the blessings that come from creating a home filled with love, respect, and faith. It encourages women to build a strong foundation for their families.

7. The Role of Faithfulness:

- The woman's trust in God (Proverbs 31:30) underscores the importance of faith and dependence on God for guidance and strength.

8. The Value of a Strong Work Ethic:

- The woman's diligence and commitment to her work (Proverbs 31:13-19, 27) encourages women to embrace a strong work ethic and to strive for excellence in all their endeavors.

9. The Reward of a Life Well Lived:

- The final verse (Proverbs 31:31) celebrates the woman's accomplishments, reminding women that a life lived in accordance with God's principles is worthy of praise and honor.

Finding Your Place

Embrace the value of hard work and resourcefulness, using your skills and talents to serve your family and community. Speak with wisdom and kindness, using your words to build up and encourage others. Cultivate strength and dignity, grounded in your faith and commitment to God's principles. Extend compassion and generosity to those in need, making a difference in your community. Practice planning and preparation in your daily life, managing your responsibilities with wisdom. Create a home environment filled with love, respect, and faith. Trust in God for guidance and strength, allowing your faith to be the foundation of your actions. Embrace a strong work ethic, striving for excellence in all you do. Remember that a life lived in accordance with God's principles will be rewarded and honored.

Cultivating a Life of Prayer

Virtuous Lord, who embodies and inspires excellence, thank You for the inspiring portrait of the woman of noble character. Help me to embrace the values of hard work, kindness, and generosity. Empower me to be a source of strength and encouragement to those around me. Grant me wisdom in managing my responsibilities and faithfulness in seeking Your guidance. May my home be a place of love and faith, reflecting Your presence. Inspire me to use my gifts and talents to make a difference in the world, leaving a legacy that honors You. In Jesus' name, Amen.

Week 21: Ecclesiastes - Women's Wisdom in a World of Vanity

Meet: The Teacher, Exploring Life's Meaning

The book of Ecclesiastes, traditionally attributed to King Solomon, presents a contemplative exploration of life's meaning and purpose in a world often marked by vanity and fleeting pleasures. The author, known as "The Teacher" or "Qoheleth," reflects on the futility of human pursuits that are detached from God. Through a series of observations and introspective musings, he grapples with the complexities of life "under the sun," ultimately concluding that true meaning and satisfaction are found in fearing God and embracing the simple joys He provides.

While the book doesn't explicitly focus on women, its wisdom and insights resonate deeply with women navigating the challenges and complexities of life. The Teacher's search for meaning encourages women to look beyond superficial pursuits and to find lasting fulfillment in a relationship with God, embracing the present moment with gratitude and wisdom.

Lessons Learned

1. The Futility of Worldly Pursuits:
   - Ecclesiastes 1:2 states, "Meaningless! Meaningless! Everything is meaningless!" This stark declaration prompts women to recognize that pursuing wealth, pleasure, or fame without God ultimately leads to emptiness.

2. The Importance of Contentment:
   - Ecclesiastes 5:10 reminds us, "Whoever loves money never has enough." This encourages women to find contentment in

what they have, rather than constantly striving for more, recognizing the value of gratitude.

3. The Seasons of Life:
   - Ecclesiastes 3:1-8 emphasizes that there is a time for everything under heaven. It teaches women to embrace the different seasons of life, accepting both joy and sorrow as part of God's plan.

4. The Value of Relationships:
   - Ecclesiastes 4:9-12 highlights the benefits of companionship and the support found in relationships. It encourages women to foster meaningful connections and build strong communities.

5. The Significance of Work:
   - While acknowledging the toil associated with work (Ecclesiastes 2:22-23), the Teacher also recognizes the value of finding purpose and satisfaction in one's labor.

6. The Gift of Joy:
   - Ecclesiastes 9:7-9 encourages embracing life's simple joys, suggesting that finding happiness in everyday moments is a gift from God.

7. The Reality of Death:
   - Ecclesiastes 3:19-20 reminds us of the brevity of life and the inevitability of death. This perspective encourages women to live purposefully, making the most of the time they have been given.

8. The Mystery of God's Ways:
   - The Teacher acknowledges the limitations of human understanding (Ecclesiastes 8:16-17), encouraging women to trust in God's wisdom and sovereignty, even when His ways seem unclear.

9. The Importance of Fearing God:
   - Ecclesiastes 12:13-14 concludes with the ultimate lesson: "Fear God and keep his commandments, for this is the duty of all mankind." It emphasizes that true meaning in life is found in a relationship with God.

Finding Your Place

Recognize that true fulfillment in life comes from a relationship with God, not from chasing fleeting pleasures or material possessions. Cultivate contentment and gratitude for the blessings in your life. Embrace the different seasons of life, accepting the challenges and joys that each season brings. Invest in building meaningful relationships and fostering a strong community. Find purpose and satisfaction in your work, using your talents and skills to contribute to the world around you. Celebrate the simple joys of life, appreciating the gifts God has given you. Live with purpose, knowing that time is precious and life is a gift. Trust in God's wisdom and sovereignty, even when His ways seem mysterious. Make fearing God and keeping His commandments the foundation of your life.

Cultivating a Life of Prayer

Eternal God, who provides purpose and meaning, You are the source of all meaning and purpose. Help me to see beyond the vanity of this world and to find true fulfillment in You. Teach me to embrace the seasons of my life with grace and to value the relationships that bring me joy. Guide me to find purpose in my work and to celebrate the simple blessings You provide. May my life reflect a deep reverence for You, as I seek to live in obedience to Your commands. In Jesus' name, Amen.

Week 22: Song of Solomon - Love and Desire

Meet: Love and Desire

The Song of Solomon, also known as the Song of Songs, is a poetic exploration of love and desire between a bride and her bridegroom. Traditionally attributed to King Solomon, this book uses rich imagery and metaphor to celebrate romantic and physical love within the context of a committed relationship.

The text is often interpreted as an allegory of the love between Christ and the Church, though it is also appreciated for its straightforward depiction of the beauty and intensity of human love. The Song of Solomon highlights the themes of passion, longing, and the joy of romantic connection, portraying love as a powerful and divine gift.

Lessons Learnt

1. The Beauty of Romantic Love
   - The Song of Solomon celebrates the beauty and depth of romantic love. It shows that love, when expressed within a committed relationship, is a gift from God and a source of joy.

2. The Importance of Intimacy
   - Intimacy, both emotional and physical, is highlighted as a vital component of a loving relationship. The book emphasizes the significance of closeness and connection in deepening love.

3. The Role of Desire in Love
   - Desire is portrayed as a natural and integral part of romantic love. The Song of Solomon teaches that healthy desire within the bounds of marriage is a positive aspect of love.

4. The Value of Mutual Respect
   - The relationship depicted in the Song of Solomon is characterized by mutual respect and admiration. This underscores the importance of honoring and valuing each other in a relationship.

5. The Celebration of Physical Affection
   - The book's vivid imagery celebrates physical affection as an expression of love. It teaches that physical touch, when shared with respect and within the confines of a loving relationship, is a meaningful expression of love.

6. The Joy of Emotional Connection
   - Beyond physical attraction, the emotional connection between the lovers is deeply valued. The Song of Solomon highlights the joy that comes from a strong emotional bond.

7. The Significance of Commitment
   - The relationship in the Song of Solomon is portrayed as enduring and committed. It shows that lasting love is built on a foundation of commitment and loyalty.

8. The Role of Communication
   - The exchange of heartfelt words and expressions between the lovers illustrates the importance of communication in fostering a loving relationship.

9. The Celebration of Love's Mysteries
   - The Song of Solomon embraces the mysteries and complexities of love. It encourages celebrating the unique and often ineffable aspects of romantic relationships.

Finding Your Place

Fasten to the lessons of the Song of Solomon by nurturing the emotional and physical aspects of your relationships with respect and commitment. Celebrate the beauty of love and desire within the context of a committed partnership, and communicate openly with your partner. Let your love be characterized by mutual respect, affection, and deep emotional connection. Recognize the value of desire as a positive and meaningful part of your relationship.

Cultivating a Life of Prayer

Loving God, who models and celebrates true love, I give honor to You for the gift of love and the beauty of intimate relationships. I want to honor and celebrate the romantic love I have with respect and commitment. Guide me to express love both emotionally and physically within the boundaries of Your design. May I communicate openly and deeply with my partner and appreciate the joy that comes from a committed and loving relationship. Teach me to cherish and nurture the love that You have blessed me with. In Jesus' name, Amen.

Week 23: Isaiah - The Suffering Servant and Women

Meet: The Woman Who Waits, Hope in God's Redemption

The book of Isaiah, a rich tapestry of prophecy, judgment, and hope, offers a profound message of redemption through the figure of the Suffering Servant. While the identity of the Servant is ultimately revealed as Jesus Christ, the themes of suffering, sacrifice, and restoration resonate deeply with the experiences of women throughout history.

Isaiah's prophecies, filled with imagery of comfort, healing, and a future where sorrow and oppression are replaced with joy and justice, offer a message of hope to those who have endured pain and hardship. The imagery of waiting, longing, and ultimately, rejoicing in God's deliverance, speaks directly to the hearts of women who have navigated the complexities of a broken world.

Lessons Learned

1. Comfort for the Brokenhearted:
   - Isaiah 40:1-2 emphasizes God's compassion for His people and His desire to comfort those who mourn. This reminds women that God sees their pain and offers solace and strength in times of grief.

2. Hope for the Future:
   - Isaiah 40:31 speaks of those who hope in the Lord renewing their strength. It encourages women to maintain hope, even in difficult circumstances, trusting that God will provide strength and renewal.

3. The Beauty of Redemption:

- Isaiah 52:7 describes the beauty of the feet of those who bring good news. This imagery points to the beauty and hope that comes with God's redemption, offering a vision of a transformed future.

4. The Power of Waiting:

- Throughout Isaiah, the theme of waiting for God's deliverance is prominent (Isaiah 40:31, 61:1-3). It teaches women the importance of patience and trust in God's timing, even when waiting seems long.

5. God's Justice for the Oppressed:

- Isaiah 61:1-2 proclaims God's commitment to justice for the oppressed. It reminds women that God sees injustice and will act to bring about righteousness.

6. The Healing Power of God:

- Isaiah 53:5 speaks of being healed by the Servant's wounds. It points to the ultimate healing and restoration that comes through Jesus Christ, offering hope for wholeness and renewal.

7. The Significance of Bearing Burdens:

- The Suffering Servant's willingness to bear the burdens of others (Isaiah 53:4-6) encourages women to embrace compassion and empathy, supporting those who are hurting.

8. The Strength Found in God:

- Isaiah 40:29-31 reminds us that God gives strength to the weary. It empowers women to rely on God's strength, especially when they feel weak or discouraged.

9. The Joy of Restoration:

- Isaiah 61:10-11 describes the joy of being clothed with garments of salvation. It invites women to embrace the joy of God's redemption and the beauty of a transformed life.

Finding Your Place

Embrace God's comfort and find solace in His presence, especially during times of grief and hardship. Hold onto hope for a brighter future, trusting in God's promises of restoration and renewal. Recognize the beauty of God's redemption and the hope it brings to a broken world. Practice patience and trust in God's timing, knowing that He is working all things together for your good. Stand up for justice and advocate for the oppressed, knowing that God is on the side of righteousness. Seek healing from your wounds, both physical and emotional, through the power of Jesus Christ. Extend compassion and empathy to those who are hurting, offering support and encouragement. Rely on God's strength when you are weak or discouraged, knowing that He will sustain you. Embrace the joy of God's redemption, allowing it to transform your life and bring you true fulfillment.

Cultivating a Life of Prayer

Compassionate Savior, who understands and redeems, thank You for the promise of redemption through Jesus Christ. Help me to find solace in Your presence when I am hurting and to trust in Your power to heal and restore. Grant me the patience to wait for Your timing, and fill me with a steadfast hope for a brighter future. Empower me to be an advocate for justice and to show compassion to those in need. May I embrace the joy of Your redemption and reflect Your love and grace in all I do. In Jesus' name, Amen.

Week 24: Jeremiah - The Women Mourners: Voices of Lament

Meet: The Women of Jerusalem, Grieving a Lost City

The book of Jeremiah, a poignant record of Judah's decline and eventual fall to Babylon, is filled with laments and expressions of grief over the destruction of Jerusalem and the exile of its people. While Jeremiah himself is known as the "weeping prophet," the book also highlights the voices of women who mourn the loss of their beloved city, their homes, and their way of life.

These women, often unnamed, stand as powerful symbols of the collective grief and trauma experienced by the nation. Their lamentations, filled with anguish and despair, give voice to the pain of loss and displacement, offering a raw and honest portrayal of the emotional and spiritual impact of national tragedy.

Lessons Learned

1. The Validity of Lament:
   - The women's lamentations (Jeremiah 9:17-20) demonstrate the importance of acknowledging and expressing grief. It teaches women that it is healthy and necessary to grieve loss.

2. The Communal Nature of Grief:
   - The collective mourning of the women (Jeremiah 9:17-20) highlights the shared experience of grief and the importance of finding solace and support in community.

3. The Impact of War and Violence:
   - The lamentations vividly describe the devastation and suffering caused by war (Lamentations 2:11-12), reminding

women of the devastating consequences of violence and conflict.

4. The Depth of Emotional Pain:
   - The raw and honest expressions of anguish and despair (Lamentations 1:1-22) acknowledge the depth of emotional pain experienced during times of loss and trauma.

5. The Importance of Remembrance:
   - The women's lamentations serve as a testament to the importance of remembering and honoring the past, even in the midst of pain and sorrow.

6. The Role of Faith in Lament:
   - Even in their deepest despair, the women still acknowledge God (Lamentations 3:22-24), demonstrating that lament does not negate faith but can be a pathway to deeper trust.

7. The Hope for Restoration:
   - Embedded within the lamentations are glimpses of hope for restoration and future redemption (Lamentations 3:25-26), reminding women that God's love and faithfulness endure even in the darkest times.

8. The Strength of Vulnerability:
   - The women's willingness to openly express their grief (Lamentations 1:1-22) illustrates the strength found in vulnerability and the power of sharing one's pain with others.

9. The Healing Power of Time:
   - While acknowledging the deep pain of the present, the lamentations also hint at the healing power of time and the possibility of finding solace and strength in the future (Lamentations 3:21-26).

Finding Your Place

Recognize the validity of your own grief and the importance of expressing it openly and honestly. Seek comfort and support in your community, sharing your burdens with others who understand your pain. Acknowledge the impact of violence and conflict, working toward peace and reconciliation in your own life and in the world around you. Allow yourself to feel the depth of your emotions, understanding that grief is a natural response to loss. Remember and honor the past, finding ways to commemorate and learn from experiences of sorrow. Maintain your faith in God, even when you are struggling to understand His ways. Find hope in God's promises of restoration and renewal, believing in His ability to heal broken hearts. Embrace vulnerability as a source of strength, allowing yourself to connect with others on a deeper level. Trust in the healing power of time, allowing yourself to grieve and heal at your own pace, knowing that God is with you every step of the way.

Cultivating a Life of Prayer

Comforting God, who soothes and heals broken hearts, and also weeps with those who weep, help me to grieve my losses fully and honestly. Grant me the courage to express my pain and to find solace in the support of my community. Teach me to remember the past with both sorrow and hope, holding onto Your promises of restoration. Strengthen my faith in the midst of my grief, reminding me of Your unwavering love and faithfulness. Guide me towards healing and renewal, granting peace and strength to my broken heart. In Jesus' name, Amen.

Week 25: Lamentations - Women's Grief and Hope

Meet: The Women of Jerusalem, Bearing the Weight of Loss

The book of Lamentations, attributed to the Prophet Jeremiah, offers a poignant exploration of grief, loss, and hope following the destruction of Jerusalem by the Babylonian army. The city's destruction is portrayed as a devastating blow to its inhabitants, particularly the women who are left to grapple with the immense sorrow and despair that accompany such a cataclysmic event.

Though not explicitly named, the women of Jerusalem emerge as powerful voices in Lamentations, expressing their pain and longing through a series of mournful poems. Their lamentations, filled with raw emotion, serve as a testament to the depth of grief that can accompany loss and the importance of finding hope amidst seemingly insurmountable challenges.

Lessons Learned

1. The Honesty of Lament:
   - Lamentations 1:1-22 exemplifies the raw and honest expression of grief. It teaches women that acknowledging and expressing their emotions is a vital part of the healing process.

2. The Communal Nature of Grief:
   - The collective mourning depicted in Lamentations highlights the importance of sharing grief with others. It reminds women that they are not alone in their struggles and that finding support in community is vital for healing.

3. The Depth of Despair:

- The vivid imagery and emotional depth of the lamentations (Lamentations 1:1-22) reveal the depths of despair that can accompany great loss. It encourages women to acknowledge the full spectrum of their emotions.

4. The Importance of Remembrance:

- The lamentations reflect on the past, remembering what has been lost and the beauty of what once was. It teaches women that remembering can be a part of the healing process.

5. The Power of Hope:

- Despite the intense sorrow, Lamentations 3:22-24 emphasizes God's unfailing faithfulness and mercy. It reminds women that even in the depths of their grief, hope is possible.

6. The Role of Faith in Healing:

- The poet's faith in God's power to restore (Lamentations 3:22-24) shows that even amidst profound loss, faith can provide strength, comfort, and a sense of purpose.

7. The Value of Patience:

- Lamentations 3:25-26 encourages patience, reminding women that God's timing for restoration and healing is different from our own.

8. The Importance of Self-Care:

- The poet's call to turn inward (Lamentations 3:28) suggests the need for self-reflection and care during times of profound grief, allowing for emotional processing and restoration.

9. The Strength in Vulnerability:

- The raw vulnerability expressed in Lamentations shows that strength can be found in openly sharing one's pain and seeking support from others.

Finding Your Place

Embrace your grief honestly, allowing yourself to experience the full spectrum of your emotions. Seek support and understanding from your community, sharing your burdens and finding solace in collective empathy. Remember and cherish the past, both the joys and sorrows, allowing them to shape your present. Hold onto the promise of God's faithfulness and mercy, even in the darkest times. Allow your faith to be your source of strength and comfort in the face of despair. Trust in God's timing for restoration, and cultivate patience as you navigate your journey of healing. Engage in self-care and nurture your emotional well-being, allowing yourself to process your pain and to seek support. Recognize the strength that comes from vulnerability, connecting with others and sharing your experiences with honesty.

Cultivating a Life of Prayer

Hopeful Healer, who brings solace and renewal, I know You understand our deepest sorrow with full honesty and hope. Guide me to process my grief fully and to find strength in Your love. Guide me to remember and cherish the past, even in its sadness, and to trust in Your faithfulness to restore what has been lost. Empower me to lean on Your promises for healing and renewal. Help me to find comfort and support in my community, and to practice self-care as I navigate my journey of grief. May I find strength in vulnerability and hope for a brighter future through Your grace. In Jesus' name, Amen.

Week 26: Ezekiel - The Vision of the Valley of Dry Bones

Meet: Ezekiel, the Prophet of Hope

Ezekiel, a priest and prophet, receives his calling during the Babylonian exile, a time of immense suffering and displacement for the Israelites. Known for his vivid and often symbolic visions, Ezekiel's ministry focuses on bringing messages of hope and restoration to a people facing despair.

The vision of the Valley of Dry Bones (Ezekiel 37:1-14) is one of the most powerful and iconic in the book of Ezekiel. This vision, filled with imagery of resurrection and renewal, serves as a powerful metaphor for God's ability to bring new life and hope to seemingly hopeless situations. It encourages believers to trust in God's power to restore, to believe in the possibility of transformation, and to look beyond immediate circumstances to the promises of God's ultimate plan.

Lessons Learned

1. God's Power to Restore:

   - The vision of the dry bones coming back to life (Ezekiel 37:1-14) demonstrates God's power to bring restoration and renewal, even in seemingly impossible circumstances. It reminds women that God's power can overcome even the most daunting challenges.

2. The Promise of New Life:

   - The breath of life breathed into the dry bones (Ezekiel 37:5-10) symbolizes the transformative power of God's Spirit, offering hope for a new beginning and a renewed life in Christ.

3. The Importance of Trust:

- The prophet's reliance on God's guidance in interpreting the vision (Ezekiel 37:11-14) emphasizes the importance of trusting God's word and His plans, even when they seem incomprehensible.

4. The Hope for a Future Restoration:

- The vision of the dry bones coming to life points towards a future restoration of God's people and the promise of a renewed world.

5. God's Sovereignty Over All:

- The prophet's assertion that God has authority over all things (Ezekiel 37:12-14) reminds women of God's ultimate control and power to work out His plans.

6. The Power of God's Word:

- The prophet's proclamation of God's word (Ezekiel 37:11-14) emphasizes the transformative power of God's words and the importance of listening to and obeying them.

7. The Value of Community in Renewal:

- The vision of a united community (Ezekiel 37:11-14) highlights the importance of unity and collective action in experiencing God's work of restoration.

8. The Role of the Spirit in Revival:

- The breath of life breathed into the bones symbolizes the work of the Holy Spirit, demonstrating the power of the Spirit in bringing about spiritual renewal and transformation.

9. God's Compassion for His People:

- The vision of the dry bones coming to life reminds women that God desires to restore His people and that His heart is full of compassion for their needs.

Finding Your Place

Trust in God's power to bring restoration and renewal, even in seemingly impossible circumstances. Embrace the hope of new life in Christ, believing that God can transform your life and your world. Rely on God's word as a source of guidance and truth, and trust in His sovereignty and control over all things. Look forward to a future of restoration and redemption, holding onto God's promises for a renewed world. Recognize and celebrate the work of the Holy Spirit in your life, allowing Him to guide and empower you. Seek unity and support within your community, working together to bring about God's plan for restoration. Trust in God's love and compassion, knowing that He desires to heal and restore His people.

Cultivating a Life of Prayer

Reviving Spirit, who breathes life into desolate places and into all things, thank You for the powerful vision of the valley of dry bones. Help me to trust in Your power to bring restoration and renewal, even when circumstances seem hopeless. Fill me with hope for a brighter future, believing in Your promises for a new creation. Guide me to rely on Your word and to trust in Your sovereignty over all things. Empower me to embrace the work of Your Holy Spirit in my life, and to be a part of building Your kingdom. Remind me of Your love and compassion for Your people, and help me to live in anticipation of Your glorious restoration. In Jesus' name, Amen.

Week 27: Daniel - Susanna: Maintaining Integrity Under False Accusation

Meet: Susanna, a Woman of Faith and Courage

The story of Susanna, a faithful woman wrongfully accused and facing a potential death sentence, unfolds in the book of Daniel. Despite her innocence and righteousness, Susanna is targeted by two corrupt elders, who falsely accuse her of immorality and seek to exploit her vulnerability.

Susanna's story highlights the power of faith in the face of injustice and the strength needed to stand firm against false accusations. Her unwavering commitment to truth and her courageous defense before her accusers are powerful reminders that God sees the unseen and will ultimately vindicate the righteous.

Lessons Learned

1. The Importance of Integrity:

   - Susanna's steadfast commitment to righteousness (Daniel 13:1-5) demonstrates the importance of maintaining moral purity and integrity, even when facing temptations or accusations.

2. The Power of Prayer:

   - Susanna's prayer for deliverance (Daniel 13:42-45) illustrates the effectiveness of seeking God's intervention in times of crisis, emphasizing the power of prayer for protection and guidance.

3. The Dangers of False Accusations:

- The elders' deceitful attempt to frame Susanna (Daniel 13:17-23) highlights the dangers of false accusations and the power they can wield over vulnerable individuals.

4. The Courage to Stand Firm:

- Susanna's bravery in defending herself (Daniel 13:24-27) shows the importance of standing firm for truth, even when facing powerful adversaries.

5. The Role of Wisdom and Discernment:

- Daniel's wisdom in exposing the elders' lies (Daniel 13:29-46) illustrates the importance of discernment and wisdom in recognizing truth and justice.

6. The Power of God's Justice:

- God's intervention in Susanna's trial (Daniel 13:45-50) demonstrates His commitment to justice, assuring women that He will ultimately vindicate the innocent.

7. The Impact of a Faithful Witness:

- Susanna's steadfast faith in God's justice inspires others and strengthens their belief in God's power to defend the righteous.

8. The Importance of Seeking Justice:

- Susanna's story encourages women to seek justice when facing injustice, reminding them that God is a God of justice and will uphold those who seek Him.

9. The Strength of Women:

- Susanna's courage and resilience in the face of false accusations highlight the strength and determination found in women of faith.

Finding Your Place

Uphold integrity in your actions and choices, remaining steadfast in your commitment to righteousness. Cultivate a strong prayer life, seeking God's intervention and guidance in times of need. Be cautious of false accusations, trusting in your own sense of right and wrong. Stand firm in truth, defending yourself against injustice with courage and resolve. Develop wisdom and discernment to recognize deceit and to speak truth to those in power. Trust in God's justice, knowing He will ultimately uphold righteousness. Find strength in your faith and in your relationship with God, drawing on His power to guide and protect you. Seek justice when you experience injustice, standing up for your rights and for those who are vulnerable. Remember that God is your defender and that you possess inner strength, even in the face of challenges.

Cultivating a Life of Prayer

Faithful Deliverer, who saves and strengthens in trials, show me how to maintain my integrity, even in the face of temptation or accusation. Guide me to seek Your wisdom and protection in my life, and to trust in Your unwavering justice. Grant me courage to speak truth to power and to stand firm in my beliefs. May I be a voice for the innocent and a defender of righteousness. Strengthen my faith and fill me with a confident hope in Your power to work for justice and to vindicate the oppressed. In Jesus' name, Amen.

Week 28: Hosea - Gomer, the Unfaithful Wife

Meet: Gomer, A Reflection of Israel's Unfaithfulness

Gomer, the wife of the prophet Hosea, plays a central role in the book of Hosea, serving as a living parable of God's relationship with Israel. Her story is both tragic and hopeful, marked by her unfaithfulness to her husband and her eventual redemption. While Gomer's actions often reflect the spiritual unfaithfulness of Israel through idolatry and disobedience, her journey ultimately emphasizes God's unwavering love, His persistent pursuit of His people, and the possibility of forgiveness and restoration.

For women, Gomer's story can be a difficult one to navigate. Her choices and her vulnerability make her a complex and relatable figure, prompting reflection on the nature of love, commitment, and the consequences of straying from one's path. Ultimately, Gomer's journey highlights the healing power of God's love and the hope that exists for a renewed relationship with Him.

Lessons Learned

1. The Pain of Unfaithfulness:
   - Gomer's unfaithfulness to Hosea (Hosea 1:2-3) mirrors Israel's unfaithfulness to God. It teaches women the devastating consequences of betrayal and broken commitments in relationships.

2. God's Unconditional Love:
   - Despite Gomer's unfaithfulness, Hosea continues to love her (Hosea 3:1-3). It demonstrates God's unconditional love for His people, even when they turn away from Him.

3. The Depth of God's Forgiveness:

   - Hosea's willingness to redeem and restore Gomer (Hosea 3:1-3) reveals the depth of God's forgiveness and His desire for reconciliation with His people, offering hope for restoration.

4. The Consequences of Our Choices:

   - Gomer's experiences highlight the consequences of her actions (Hosea 2:5-13). It reminds women that choices have repercussions, both for themselves and for those around them.

5. The Power of Redemption:

   - God's promise to redeem and restore Israel (Hosea 14:4-8) offers a message of hope and transformation. It encourages women to trust in God's power to bring about redemption, even in difficult situations.

6. The Importance of Faithfulness:

   - Hosea's faithful love for Gomer, even in the midst of her unfaithfulness, serves as a testament to the importance of commitment and dedication in relationships.

7. Recognizing Our Need for God:

   - Gomer's vulnerability and her need for rescue (Hosea 2:14-15) reflect the human condition of needing God's grace and guidance.

8. Responding to God's Call:

   - Hosea's willingness to obey God's command to marry Gomer (Hosea 1:2-3) teaches the importance of responding to God's call, even when it's challenging or unconventional.

9. The Transforming Power of Love:

   - Gomer's eventual return to Hosea (Hosea 3:1-3) illustrates the transformative power of love and forgiveness, offering hope for healing and renewal.

Finding Your Place

Recognize the importance of faithfulness in relationships and the pain caused by broken commitments. Understand and embrace the reality of God's unconditional love for you, even when you make mistakes. Remember that God's forgiveness is always available, and He desires reconciliation with you. Be mindful of the consequences of your choices and strive to live a life that honors God's standards. Trust in God's power to redeem and restore your life, bringing healing and hope to broken situations. Learn from the example of Hosea's faithful love and seek to embody that same love in your relationships. Acknowledge your need for God's grace and guidance. Be courageous in responding to God's call on your life, even if it seems challenging. Believe in the transformative power of love and forgiveness to bring about healing and a fresh start.

Cultivating a Life of Prayer

Loving Forgiver, who restores faithfulness and love, and whose love never fails, thank You for revealing the depth of Your love and mercy. Help me to understand and experience Your unconditional love, and to extend that same love to others. Grant me the courage to forgive those who have wronged me and to seek restoration in my relationships. Teach me to recognize the consequences of my actions, and to choose paths that lead to a deeper relationship with You. Fill me with hope for redemption, trusting in Your power to heal and renew. May my life be a testament to Your grace and love. In Jesus' name, Amen.

Week 29: Joel - Your Daughters Will Prophesy

Meet: The Daughters of Zion, Empowered by the Spirit

The book of Joel, a message of warning and hope for the nation of Judah, contains a remarkable prophecy concerning the outpouring of God's Spirit in the last days. Joel 2:28-29 declares, "And afterward, I will pour out my Spirit on all people. Your sons and daughters will prophesy, your old men will dream dreams, your young men will see visions." This prophetic declaration transcends gender and age, offering a vision of God's Spirit empowering all people to participate in His redemptive work.

This passage, often referred to as the "Pentecost Prophecy," emphasizes the transformative power of the Holy Spirit and the inclusion of women in ministry and leadership. It inspires women, especially young women, to embrace their spiritual gifts, to speak God's truth boldly, and to contribute to the advancement of His Kingdom.

Lessons Learned

1. The Promise of the Spirit:
   - Joel's prophecy (Joel 2:28-29) emphasizes that God's Spirit will be poured out on all people, regardless of gender or age. This assures women that they, too, are recipients of God's empowering presence.

2. The Gift of Prophecy:
   - The specific mention of daughters prophesying challenges traditional views and affirms that women are called to speak God's truth and to minister within the community.

3. The Diversity of Spiritual Gifts:
   - The prophecy lists various manifestations of the Spirit, including prophecy, dreams, and visions, emphasizing the diversity of gifts given to believers.

4. The Empowerment for Service:
   - The outpouring of the Spirit is linked to God's restoration and the renewal of His people (Joel 2:23-27). It highlights the empowerment given to believers for service and ministry.

5. Breaking Down Barriers:
   - The inclusion of all people in this prophecy breaks down traditional gender roles and social barriers, illustrating God's desire to use everyone for His purposes.

6. The Importance of Listening to God's Voice:
   - The mention of dreams and visions underscores the importance of listening for God's voice in different ways and being sensitive to His leading.

7. The Role of Women in the End Times:
   - Joel's prophecy suggests a significant role for women in proclaiming God's message and participating in the events leading to the Day of the Lord.

8. The Call to Boldness:
   - The act of prophesying requires boldness and courage, inspiring women to speak God's truth with conviction and without fear.

9. Empowerment for Transformation:
   - The ultimate purpose of the Spirit's outpouring is to transform lives and bring about God's kingdom. This emphasizes the transformative power of God's Spirit at work in and through believers.

Finding Your Place

Embrace the promise of the Holy Spirit and welcome His presence in your life. Recognize the gifts and talents God has given you, including the gift of prophecy, and use them for His glory. Understand that you are called to serve and minister, breaking down any barriers that limit your participation in God's kingdom. Actively seek to hear God's voice through prayer, dreams, and Scripture. Believe that God desires to use you in powerful ways, especially in sharing His truth and advancing His work. Be bold and courageous in proclaiming God's message, trusting in the power of the Holy Spirit to guide and equip you. Live a life that reflects the transformative power of God's Spirit, allowing Him to work through you to impact your community.

Cultivating a Life of Prayer

Prophetic Voice, who reveals Your plans and promises, thank You for pouring out Your Spirit on all people, including Your daughters. Help me to recognize and embrace the gifts You have given me, using them to serve Your purposes. Fill me with Your Spirit, empowering me to prophesy Your truth and to boldly share Your message. Guide me to hear Your voice clearly and to be sensitive to Your leading. May my life be a reflection of Your transformative power, bringing hope and renewal to those around me. In Jesus' name, Amen.

Week 30: Amos - Women of Samaria: Confronting Luxury and Social Injustice

Meet: The Women of Samaria, Living in a World of Extremes

The prophet Amos, a shepherd called by God to deliver a message of judgment and repentance to the Northern Kingdom of Israel, provides a stark critique of the social injustices prevalent in his time. While his prophecies address the nation as a whole, Amos particularly targets the wealthy women of Samaria, the capital city, for their lavish lifestyles and indifference to the suffering of the poor and oppressed.

Amos's pronouncements against the "cows of Bashan" (Amos 4:1), a metaphor for the wealthy women who live in luxury and comfort, challenge their complacency and expose their complicity in perpetuating social inequalities. This message serves as a powerful reminder for women of all generations to examine their own lives, to recognize the interconnectedness of their choices with the wellbeing of others, and to actively work towards justice and righteousness in their communities.

Lessons Learned

1. The Danger of Complacency:
   - Amos's condemnation of the women of Samaria (Amos 4:1-3) highlights the dangers of complacency and indifference to the suffering of others, particularly when one is living in privilege.

2. The Responsibility of Privilege:
   - The luxurious lifestyles of the women of Samaria, contrasted with the poverty and oppression of others, emphasizes the

responsibility that comes with privilege. It challenges women to use their resources and influence to advocate for justice.

3. The Call to Justice and Righteousness:

   - Amos's central message of justice and righteousness (Amos 5:24) applies to all members of society, urging women to actively participate in creating a fairer and more equitable world.

4. The Connection Between Faith and Action:

   - Amos's critique of empty religious rituals (Amos 5:21-24) underscores the importance of aligning faith with actions. It reminds women that true worship of God must be accompanied by a commitment to justice and righteousness.

5. The Impact of Individual Choices:

   - The women of Samaria's choices to indulge in luxury while ignoring the needs of the poor demonstrate how individual decisions can contribute to systemic injustice. It encourages women to consider the impact of their choices on those around them.

6. The Power of Prophetic Voices:

   - Amos's willingness to confront the wealthy and powerful (Amos 4:1-3) highlights the role of prophetic voices in challenging injustice and speaking truth to power.

7. The Consequences of Injustice:

   - Amos's prophecies of judgment (Amos 7:7-9) serve as a warning about the consequences of ignoring the cries of the oppressed and perpetuating injustice.

8. The Hope for Transformation:

   - Despite the harsh pronouncements of judgment, Amos also offers hope for repentance and transformation (Amos 5:4-6, 9:11-15), reminding women that change is possible when we turn back to God and His ways.

9. The Call to Action:
   - Amos's message is a call to action, urging women to take responsibility for creating a more just and equitable society, demonstrating their faith through deeds of compassion and justice.

Finding Your Place

Be mindful of the dangers of complacency and indifference, especially if you have been blessed with privilege. Recognize the responsibility you have to use your resources and influence to advocate for justice and equality. Commit to living out your faith through actions that promote righteousness and fairness. Challenge empty religious practices and seek to align your worship with a deep concern for justice and compassion. Consider the impact of your choices on others, understanding that your decisions can contribute to or alleviate injustice. Be inspired by the courage of prophetic voices, speaking out against injustice and advocating for change. Remember that God will hold individuals and communities accountable for their actions. Hold onto the hope that transformation is possible through repentance and a commitment to God's ways. Take action to create a more just and equitable world, reflecting God's love and mercy in your community.

Cultivating a Life of Prayer

Righteous God, who hears the cries of the oppressed, help me to recognize and reject complacency in my own life, and to be sensitive to the suffering of those around me. Empower me to act justly and to use my resources to advocate for those who are marginalized. Inspire me to live out my faith authentically, combining worship with a commitment to righteousness and compassion. May my choices reflect Your love and justice, working towards a world where all people are treated with dignity and fairness. In Jesus' name, Amen.

Week 31: Obadiah - Women in Edom: Surviving National Calamity

Meet: The Women of Edom, Facing National Destruction

The book of Obadiah, the shortest book in the Bible, delivers a powerful prophecy of judgment against the nation of Edom for their betrayal and cruelty towards their brother nation, Israel. Though the book primarily focuses on the fall of Edom, it implicitly addresses the impact of this national calamity on Edomite women, who are left to endure the devastating consequences of their nation's actions.

The story of Edom serves as a reminder of the dangers of pride, the consequences of violence, and the importance of remaining faithful to God's principles. For women, Obadiah's message provides a poignant reflection on the resilience and strength required to navigate through times of hardship and loss. It emphasizes the importance of looking beyond the immediate tragedy and finding hope in God's promises.

Lessons Learned

1. The Consequences of Pride and Violence:
   - Obadiah 1:3-4 highlights the consequences of Edom's pride and their actions against Israel. It teaches women that arrogance and violence lead to downfall and judgment, reminding them to live with humility and compassion.

2. The Importance of Seeking Refuge in God:
   - Obadiah's message of judgment serves as a reminder to seek refuge in God during times of trouble and turmoil, demonstrating that God's protection is available to those who trust in Him.

3. Hope for Restoration:

- Despite the prophecy of judgment, Obadiah 1:17-21 offers a glimmer of hope for the restoration of Israel. It encourages women to believe in God's promise for a future of renewal.

4. The Impact of Betrayal:

- Edom's betrayal of Israel highlights the consequences of broken relationships and the importance of remaining faithful and loyal to those in need.

5. The Strength of Faith in Adversity:

- Obadiah's prophecy, while focused on judgment, implicitly acknowledges the strength and resilience of those who remain faithful through hardship. It encourages women to trust in God's promises and to find hope amidst suffering.

6. The Role of Women in National Trauma:

- While the book primarily focuses on the nation's destruction, it implicitly addresses the impact of this trauma on Edomite women. It reminds women that they are not immune to the consequences of societal actions and that they too must find ways to cope and heal.

7. The Importance of Forgiving Others:

- While not explicitly mentioned, the message of Obadiah points toward the ultimate possibility of forgiveness and restoration for both Edom and Israel. It teaches women the importance of extending forgiveness and seeking reconciliation in their own relationships.

8. The Universality of God's Justice:

- Obadiah's message demonstrates that God's judgment is not confined to a particular nation but applies to all individuals and societies, challenging women to live in light of this reality.

9. The Call to Choose Love Over Hate:
   - Obadiah's stark depiction of Edom's hatred towards Israel serves as a contrast to the teachings of Christ, inspiring women to choose love over hate, compassion over judgment.

Finding Your Place

Guard against pride, cultivating humility and striving for integrity in your relationships. Seek refuge and comfort in God during times of difficulty, trusting in His promises and protection. Embrace forgiveness as a pathway to healing and reconciliation. Recognize the consequences of betrayal and strive to be faithful and loyal in your relationships. Find strength in your faith, allowing it to sustain you through challenging circumstances. Acknowledge the impact of collective actions on individuals and communities, seeking to promote peace and understanding. Choose to love rather than hate, reflecting God's mercy and grace in your interactions with others.

Cultivating a Life of Prayer

Righteous Arbiter, who executes justice on evil, continue to remind me of the consequences of pride and the importance of choosing love. Help me to cultivate humility and to seek Your refuge during times of difficulty. Teach me to extend forgiveness and to remain loyal to those who are in need. Fill my heart with compassion and guide me to embrace Your call for peace and reconciliation. May I reflect Your love in all my relationships and be a source of hope for those who are hurting. In Jesus' name, Amen.

Week 32: Jonah - The Women of Nineveh: Their Part in Repentance

Meet: The Women of Nineveh, Embracing a New Path

The book of Jonah recounts the story of the reluctant prophet Jonah who is sent by God to preach repentance to the people of Nineveh, a city known for its wickedness. While the focus is on Jonah's journey of disobedience and eventual submission, the story also implicitly addresses the impact of his message on the women of Nineveh.

Their response to Jonah's proclamation, demonstrating a collective willingness to turn from their wicked ways and seek God's mercy, highlights the significant role women play in shaping a community's spiritual direction. The story of Nineveh's repentance challenges the notion that women are merely passive participants in societal change, illustrating their agency and influence in shaping a community's trajectory towards faith and transformation.

Lessons Learned

1. The Power of Repentance:
   - The response of the people of Nineveh, including its women (Jonah 3:5-10), demonstrates that genuine repentance can lead to transformation, inspiring young women to embrace the path of turning back to God.

2. The Importance of Humility:
   - The Ninevites, including their queen, humbled themselves before God (Jonah 3:6), highlighting the importance of humility in seeking God's forgiveness and guidance.

3. The Call for Collective Change:

   - The collective action of the Ninevites, from the king to the common people, showcases the importance of collective action in seeking God's mercy. It encourages women to engage in community efforts that lead to spiritual renewal.

4. The Role of Women in Spiritual Awakening:

   - The story implicitly suggests the women of Nineveh played a significant role in their city's repentance. This highlights the influence women can have in shaping a community's spiritual journey.

5. The Value of Listening:

   - The Ninevites listen to Jonah's message (Jonah 3:5) and respond with sincerity. It reminds women of the importance of listening attentively to God's word and to one another.

6. The Breadth of God's Mercy:

   - God's compassion for Nineveh (Jonah 4:2), extending mercy even to a nation known for its wickedness, teaches about the expansiveness of God's love and His willingness to forgive.

7. Overcoming Prejudice:

   - Jonah's initial reluctance to preach to the Ninevites (Jonah 1:3) highlights the importance of overcoming prejudice and embracing God's desire for all people to repent.

8. The Power of Prayer:

   - The collective prayer and fasting of the Ninevites (Jonah 3:7-8) demonstrate the power of prayer as a collective force for change and healing.

9. The Impact of One Person's Faithfulness:

   - Jonah's eventual obedience to God's call, despite his initial reluctance, leads to Nineveh's repentance. This reinforces the impact that one person's faithfulness can have on a community.

Finding Your Place

Embrace repentance, seeking God's forgiveness and transforming your life through a genuine turning back to Him. Practice humility in your interactions with others, recognizing that everyone is in need of God's grace. Engage in collective efforts within your community to pursue spiritual renewal, understanding that shared commitment can lead to profound change. Be a good listener, actively seeking to understand the needs and perspectives of others. Trust in God's expansive mercy, knowing that His love extends to all people, regardless of their background or past actions. Challenge prejudice and seek to embrace a broader, more inclusive view of God's love for all people. Embrace the power of prayer, both individually and as a community. Be inspired by the faithfulness of those who respond to God's calling, even when it is challenging. Remember that your actions and your faithfulness can impact the lives of others, leading to positive change.

Cultivating a Life of Prayer

Merciful God, who offers redemption and forgiveness, your love embraces all, thank You for showing Your compassion for all people. Help me to embrace repentance and to seek Your forgiveness with sincerity. Guide me to cultivate humility in my interactions with others, recognizing the need for Your grace in all our lives. Empower me to participate in communal efforts to pursue spiritual renewal. Teach me to be a good listener, seeking to understand the needs and perspectives of those around me. Remind me of Your expansive mercy and help me to overcome any prejudice in my heart. May my life reflect Your love for all people, and may my prayers contribute to the transformation of our community. In Jesus' name, Amen.

Week 33: Micah - The Mothers of Israel: Hope for Restoration

Meet: The Mothers of Israel, Embodying Resilience and Hope

The book of Micah, a prophetic call to justice and righteousness for the nation of Israel, paints a bleak picture of societal corruption, injustice, and spiritual apathy. However, within this prophetic landscape, the image of mothers emerges as a symbol of resilience, hope, and the enduring love that sustains communities even during the darkest times. Micah's message, though filled with pronouncements of judgment, ultimately points toward a future restoration and a renewed covenant relationship with God.

The prophet's words, "Who is a God like you, who pardons sin and forgives the transgression of the remnant of his inheritance? You do not stay angry forever but delight to show mercy" (Micah 7:18), resonate with the heart of a mother, who embodies forgiveness, longs for restoration, and nurtures hope for a better future.

Lessons Learned

1. Hope Amidst Despair:

- Micah's prophecies, while containing harsh pronouncements of judgment, offer a glimmer of hope for restoration (Micah 4:1-5, 7:18-20). This teaches women to cling to hope, even when surrounded by despair and difficult circumstances.

2. The Power of Forgiveness:

- Micah 7:18 highlights God's willingness to forgive and pardon. It encourages women to embrace forgiveness, both in their relationship with God and in their interactions with others.

3. The Strength of a Mother's Love:

   - The metaphor of a mother's love is often used in Scripture to describe God's compassionate heart (Isaiah 49:15). Micah's message resonates with the enduring nature of a mother's love, which perseveres through hardships and seeks the well-being of her children.

4. The Call to Justice and Mercy:

   - Micah 6:8 emphasizes acting justly, loving mercy, and walking humbly with God. It encourages women to embody these virtues in their own lives and to advocate for them within their communities.

5. The Importance of Faithfulness:

   - Despite the nation's unfaithfulness, Micah's prophecies point towards a future where a faithful remnant will remain (Micah 5:7-8). It inspires women to be faithful, even when others stray from God's ways.

6. The Longing for Peace:

   - Micah's vision of a future where swords will be beaten into plowshares (Micah 4:3) reflects the deep desire for peace that resides in the heart of a mother, who longs for harmony and security for her children.

7. The Promise of God's Presence:

   - Micah 4:5 assures the people, "For all the peoples walk each in the name of its god, but we will walk in the name of the Lord our God forever and ever." It reminds women that God's presence is a constant source of strength and hope.

8. The Role of Women in Restoration:

   - While not explicitly stated, Micah's message implicitly acknowledges the role of mothers in nurturing faith and hope within families and communities, setting the stage for future generations.

9. The Power of Prayer:
   - Micah's prophecies often take the form of prayers, suggesting the importance of communicating honestly with God and trusting in His mercy and justice.

Finding Your Place

Embrace hope, even in the midst of challenging circumstances, believing in God's promise of restoration and renewal. Practice forgiveness in your relationships, extending grace to others and seeking reconciliation. Let the example of a mother's love inspire your actions, demonstrating compassion, perseverance, and a desire for the well-being of others. Advocate for justice and mercy in your community, working towards a fairer and more compassionate world. Remain steadfast in your faith, even when others falter, becoming a source of strength and encouragement. Strive for peace and harmony in your relationships and community, reflecting God's desire for unity. Trust in God's presence as a constant source of comfort and guidance. Recognize your role in shaping future generations, nurturing faith and hope in your family and community. Engage in prayer, communicating your hopes, concerns, and desires to God.

Cultivating a Life of Prayer

God of Justice, who calls us to act justly and walk humbly, fill my heart with a deep desire for peace and justice, and help me to reflect Your love and mercy in all my interactions. Strengthen me to persevere in faith, even when I face challenges, and to trust in Your power to renew and restore my life and community. May I nurture hope in those around me, guiding them towards a brighter future grounded in Your grace and faithfulness. In Jesus' name, Amen.

Week 34: Nahum - Women in Warfare: Dealing with the Aftermath of Conflict

Meet: The Women of Nineveh, Facing the Consequences of War

The book of Nahum, a passionate prophecy of judgment against the Assyrian city of Nineveh, paints a vivid picture of God's wrath against a nation known for its cruelty and violence. While the book details Nineveh's impending destruction, it implicitly addresses the impact of this devastation on its women, who are left to grapple with the consequences of war and the aftermath of their nation's fall.

Nahum's message serves as a stark reminder that violence leads to destruction and that God ultimately holds nations accountable for their actions. The prophet's words offer a glimpse into the hardships and vulnerabilities faced by women during times of conflict, while simultaneously pointing towards the hope of restoration and redemption.

Lessons Learned

1. The Devastating Impact of Violence:
   - Nahum 3:1-7 paints a picture of Nineveh's cruelty and the destruction that will befall the city. It highlights the devastating impact of violence, reminding women of the lasting scars that war leaves behind.

2. The Need for Reconciliation and Healing:
   - While Nahum emphasizes judgment, there is an implicit call for repentance and restoration (Nahum 1:9, 2:13). This reminds women that God desires healing and reconciliation, even after devastating conflict.

3. The Strength in Resilience:

- The women of Nineveh, facing the destruction of their city and their way of life, embody resilience, demonstrating the strength found in overcoming adversity and rebuilding after hardship.

4. The Importance of Community:

- The collective mourning and loss experienced by the women of Nineveh (Nahum 2:11) highlights the need for communal support and empathy during times of crisis.

5. The Power of Prayer in Times of Trouble:

- The book of Nahum, while primarily focused on judgment, reminds women of the power of prayer to seek God's comfort and protection during difficult times.

6. The Hope of a Renewed Future:

- The prophet's message, while describing judgment, also includes a glimmer of hope for a future where God's presence and grace will bring healing and restoration.

7. The Role of Women in Restoring a Nation:

- Though not explicitly stated, women will play a crucial role in the rebuilding and restoration of the nation following the devastation.

8. The Importance of Standing Against Injustice:

- Nahum's prophecy against Nineveh serves as a reminder that God opposes injustice and encourages women to advocate for peace and compassion.

9. Trusting in God's Sovereignty:

- Nahum's message emphasizes God's ultimate control over nations and events, reminding women to trust in His sovereignty and His plan for the future.

Finding Your Place

Be mindful of the destructive consequences of violence and conflict, working to promote peace and understanding. Seek comfort and solace in God's presence during times of turmoil and hardship, trusting in His love and protection. Embrace resilience and draw strength from your faith to navigate challenges and to rebuild after loss. Foster strong community ties, providing support and empathy to those who are suffering. Embrace the power of prayer as a source of strength and comfort, knowing that God hears your cries. Find hope in God's promises of restoration and healing, trusting in His plan for a brighter future. Recognize your role in contributing to the rebuilding and restoration of your community after conflict. Advocate for justice and compassion, challenging those who perpetuate violence and injustice. Trust in God's sovereignty, knowing that He is in control, even in times of turmoil.

Cultivating a Life of Prayer

Avenging God, who executes judgment against the wicked, show me to understand the devastating consequences of violence and to advocate for peace and reconciliation in my world. Strengthen me to remain steadfast in my faith during difficult times, trusting in Your comfort and protection. Inspire me to be a source of support for those who are suffering, and to build strong, caring communities. Guide me towards a future filled with Your restoration and peace, trusting in Your sovereignty and love. In Jesus' name, Amen.

Week 35: Habakkuk - Habakkuk's Prayer: Finding Strength in Troubled Times

Meet: Habakkuk, the Prophet Who Questions

Habakkuk, whose name means "embraced" or "wrestler," is a prophet who engages in a direct and honest dialogue with God in his book. His prophetic journey is marked by questions, doubts, and a deep longing for understanding. As he witnesses the rampant injustice and violence in Judah, he cries out to God, seeking to understand why the wicked seem to prosper while the righteous suffer.

Habakkuk's story provides a powerful model for navigating difficult times, reminding us that it is okay to wrestle with God, to bring our questions and doubts before Him, and to trust in His ultimate wisdom and sovereignty. His example encourages believers to find strength and hope in God's promises, even when life seems confusing and unjust.

Lessons Learned

1. The Importance of Honest Questions:

   - Habakkuk 1:2-4 demonstrates the value of bringing our honest questions and doubts to God, acknowledging that He welcomes our vulnerability and seeks to deepen our understanding.

2. Trusting in God's Sovereignty:

   - God's response to Habakkuk (Habakkuk 1:5-11) reminds us that God's ways are higher than our ways, and His plans are often beyond our comprehension. It teaches us to trust in His ultimate wisdom, even when things seem unclear.

3. The Promise of God's Justice:

   - Habakkuk 2:4-20 affirms that God will ultimately bring about justice, even when the wicked seem to prosper. It encourages believers to hold onto hope for God's intervention and to trust in His righteous judgment.

4. The Power of Faith Amidst Trials:

   - Habakkuk 2:4 emphasizes that the righteous will live by faith. It challenges believers to trust in God's promises, even when circumstances seem contradictory.

5. Finding Joy in God:

   - Habakkuk 3:17-19 expresses joy in the midst of difficult times. It teaches young women to find their source of joy in God, not in external circumstances.

6. The Importance of Praise:

   - Habakkuk's prophetic song of praise (Habakkuk 3:1-19) demonstrates the transformative power of praising God, even in the face of adversity.

7. The Value of a Godly Perspective:

   - Habakkuk's wrestling with God encourages believers to develop a broader perspective, understanding that God's plans encompass more than we can comprehend.

8. The Importance of Perseverance:

   - Habakkuk's continued faith, despite his initial struggle, highlights the importance of persevering in our relationship with God, trusting in His promises even when it's difficult.

9. The Power of Prayer:

   - Habakkuk's dialogue with God underscores the vital role of prayer in our spiritual journey, encouraging women to engage in honest conversation with God, seeking His guidance and comfort.

Finding Your Place

Bring your questions and doubts to God honestly, recognizing that He welcomes your vulnerability and seeks to deepen your understanding. Trust in God's sovereignty, even when His ways seem mysterious or unjust. Hold onto hope for God's justice, believing in His plan to address all wrongs. Live by faith, trusting in God's promises, even when circumstances seem contradictory. Cultivate joy in your relationship with God, finding strength and hope in His presence. Express your faith through praise, offering words of gratitude and adoration to God. Embrace a broader perspective, recognizing that God's plans are far greater than you can comprehend. Persevere in your faith journey, even when it's challenging, and engage in honest dialogue with God through prayer.

Cultivating a Life of Prayer

Listening God, who responds to our cries for justice, whose ways are higher than my understanding, help me to bring my doubts and questions to You with honesty and trust. Teach me to wait patiently for Your timing, and to embrace Your plans, even when they seem unclear. Strengthen my faith to live by Your promises, even when circumstances seem contradictory. Fill me with joy in my relationship with You, and guide me in expressing my faith through praise. Grant me wisdom and perspective, recognizing the vastness of Your plan and the limits of my own understanding. May I persevere in my journey, trusting in Your faithfulness and your unwavering love. In Jesus' name, Amen.

Week 36: Zephaniah - Daughters of Zion: From Shame to Praise

Meet: The Daughters of Zion, Experiencing God's Redemption

The book of Zephaniah, a prophetic message of both judgment and hope for the nation of Judah, contains a compelling vision of restoration for the "daughters of Zion," a term often used to represent the women of Jerusalem. Zephaniah's prophecies address the nation's sin and idolatry, warning of impending judgment, but also offer a glimpse of a future filled with joy and redemption, where God's presence brings healing and transformation.

The transition from shame to praise depicted in Zephaniah's message highlights the transformative power of God's grace. It encourages women to embrace forgiveness, to relinquish the burden of past mistakes, and to step into a future defined by God's love and acceptance.

Lessons Learned

1. The Reality of God's Judgment:
   - Zephaniah's pronouncements of judgment (Zephaniah 1:14-18) serve as a reminder of the consequences of sin. It teaches women to acknowledge the seriousness of turning away from God and the need for repentance.

2. The Call to Humility and Repentance:
   - Zephaniah 2:3 encourages seeking the Lord with humility. It emphasizes the importance of recognizing our need for God and turning away from sin to experience His mercy.

3. The Promise of Restoration:
   - Zephaniah 3:14-17 speaks of a future filled with joy and restoration for God's people. It offers hope that God's plan includes healing and a renewed relationship with Him.

4. From Shame to Praise:
   - The transformation from shame to praise (Zephaniah 3:14-15) highlights the power of God's redemption. It encourages women to relinquish the burden of past mistakes and embrace the freedom found in God's forgiveness.

5. The Joy of God's Presence:
   - Zephaniah 3:17 describes God rejoicing over His people with singing. It teaches women to find joy and delight in God's presence, recognizing His love for them.

6. The Power of God's Love:
   - God's compassionate response to those who seek Him (Zephaniah 3:17) emphasizes the depth of His love and His willingness to embrace those who turn to Him.

7. The Importance of Trusting God:
   - Zephaniah's message encourages women to trust in God's plan, even during difficult times, believing that He is working for their good.

8. The Strength of Community:
   - The imagery of a restored community in Zion (Zephaniah 3:14-20) highlights the importance of belonging and finding support within a community of faith.

9. Living with Hope:
   - The prophetic vision of a future filled with joy and peace (Zephaniah 3:14-20) inspires women to live with hope, knowing that God's ultimate plan includes restoration and renewal.

Finding Your Place

Acknowledge the seriousness of sin and the need for repentance, turning back to God with a humble heart. Embrace the hope of restoration, trusting in God's promises to heal and renew. Release the shame of past mistakes and embrace the joy of God's forgiveness. Recognize the power of God's love for you and find delight in His presence. Trust in God's plan for your life, even when it seems difficult or uncertain. Seek support and encouragement within your faith community, recognizing the strength found in belonging. Live with hope for a brighter future, believing in God's power to transform your circumstances and bring about peace and joy.

Cultivating a Life of Prayer

Sovereign Lord, who promises a day of reckoning and restoration, may I embrace repentance and seek Your forgiveness, trusting in the transformative power of Your grace. Help me to find joy in Your presence, recognizing the depth of Your love for me. Guide me to trust in Your plan for my life, even when it seems unclear, and to find strength in my community. Fill me with hope for a future filled with Your peace and joy. In Jesus' name, Amen.

Week 37: Haggai - Building God's House: Women's Role in Spiritual Renewal

Meet: The Women of Jerusalem, Partners in Restoration

The book of Haggai, a post-exilic prophet, focuses on the rebuilding of the Temple in Jerusalem after the Israelites returned from Babylonian captivity. Haggai's messages urge the people to prioritize God's work, emphasizing the spiritual and communal benefits of rebuilding the Temple. While the narrative primarily focuses on the men, the book implicitly acknowledges the roles that women played in the rebuilding effort and the spiritual renewal of the community.

These women, though often unnamed, contributed to the restoration through their support of their families, their participation in the work, and their dedication to the spiritual rededication of Jerusalem. Their actions highlight the importance of women in fostering community, demonstrating their strength in times of adversity, and their commitment to God's plan for their city.

Lessons Learned

1. Prioritizing God's Work:
   - Haggai 1:4 challenges the people for living in paneled houses while the temple remains in ruins. This emphasizes the importance of prioritizing spiritual obligations over personal comfort, reminding women that serving God should be a primary focus.

2. The Power of Collective Action:
   - The community's response to Haggai's call (Haggai 1:12-14) shows the strength of unity and teamwork in achieving significant tasks. It encourages women to actively participate in community efforts.

3. The Importance of Perseverance:
   - Haggai 2:3-5 addresses those who saw the former glory of the Temple and may have been discouraged by the modest start. It teaches the value of perseverance, reminding women that even small beginnings can lead to great things.

4. God's Promises of Blessings:
   - Haggai 2:18-19 promises blessings once the people prioritize the rebuilding of the Temple. It reminds women that obedience to God brings about His favor and blessings.

5. The Role of Women in Community Building:
   - The book of Haggai, while primarily focusing on the men, implicitly acknowledges the contribution of women in rebuilding the Temple. This emphasizes the essential role women play in fostering a strong and vibrant community.

6. The Strength of Faith in Adversity:
   - The community's dedication to rebuilding, despite challenges and setbacks (Haggai 1:5-7), highlights the strength found in unwavering faith, even when faced with difficulties.

7. The Importance of Encouragement:
   - Haggai's messages serve as a source of encouragement for the people (Haggai 2:4). It reminds women to be supportive of one another and to uplift those around them.

8. The Impact of Spiritual Renewal:
   - The rebuilding of the Temple serves as a focal point for spiritual renewal within the community, emphasizing the importance of seeking a deeper connection with God.

9. The Value of Shared Purpose:
   - The collective effort to rebuild the Temple reflects the power of shared purpose, uniting individuals towards a common goal. It inspires women to find common ground and work together in building God's kingdom.

Finding Your Place

Prioritize God's work in your life, placing His will at the forefront of your decisions and actions. Engage actively in your community, contributing your skills and talents to shared endeavors. Embrace perseverance, trusting in God's promises for future growth and success, even when things seem slow. Seek to be a source of encouragement to those around you, providing support and uplifting spirits. Recognize the value of your role in building a strong and vibrant community, contributing to shared goals. Stay steadfast in your faith, drawing strength from God's presence during challenging times. Seek to deepen your connection with God through spiritual renewal and growth. Embrace shared purpose, finding unity and strength in working together with others towards a common goal.

Cultivating a Life of Prayer

Encouraging God, who motivates and strengthens and inspires us to build Your kingdom, help me to prioritize Your work in my life, seeking Your guidance in all that I do. Strengthen my commitment to serving You and to contributing to the growth of my community. Grant me perseverance in challenging times, and fill me with hope for the future. May I be a source of encouragement and support to those around me, and may my life reflect a dedication to building Your kingdom. In Jesus' name, Amen.

Week 38: Zechariah - The Flying Scroll: Women's Moral Responsibility

Meet: The Women of Jerusalem, Facing a Call to Purity

The book of Zechariah, filled with symbolic visions and prophecies of restoration, addresses the Jewish community returning from exile with a message of hope and a call to renewed faithfulness. One of the most striking visions in Zechariah is that of a flying scroll (Zechariah 5:1-4), which represents God's judgment against those who break His commandments, specifically highlighting theft and perjury.

While the vision doesn't explicitly address women, it holds significant implications for understanding their moral responsibility within the community. The concept of a curse entering the house of anyone who commits these sins underscores the importance of personal accountability and the impact of individual actions on the entire household. This calls women to examine their own lives, to pursue integrity in their relationships and commitments, and to uphold God's standards of righteousness.

Lessons Learned

1. The Seriousness of Sin:

   - The flying scroll (Zechariah 5:1-4) symbolizes the weight and consequences of sin, particularly theft and perjury. It reminds women that God takes sin seriously and holds individuals accountable for their actions.

2. Personal Responsibility:

   - The curse entering the house (Zechariah 5:4) emphasizes that individual actions have consequences that can impact others, urging women to take responsibility for their choices and their impact on their families and communities.

3. The Importance of Honesty and Integrity:
   - The focus on theft and perjury highlights the importance of honesty and integrity in all aspects of life, reminding women to live with transparency and truthfulness.

4. The Need for Repentance:
   - Although judgment is pronounced, the vision implies the possibility of repentance and turning away from sin to avoid the curse.

5. The Role of Women in Upholding Righteousness:
   - While not directly addressed, the vision challenges women to play an active role in promoting righteousness within their homes and communities, setting a standard for ethical conduct.

6. The Impact of a Godly Influence:
   - Women, as wives, mothers, and members of the community, have a significant influence on shaping the moral fabric of society.

7. The Importance of Seeking God's Forgiveness:
   - The vision of judgment serves as a reminder to seek forgiveness for sin, recognizing that God's mercy is available to those who repent.

8. Building a Home Founded on Truth:
   - The image of the curse entering the house highlights the importance of building a home environment founded on truth, integrity, and respect for God's laws.

9. Living with Integrity:
   - The vision of the flying scroll challenges women to live lives of integrity, reflecting God's standards in their actions, words, and relationships.

Finding Your Place

Recognize the seriousness of sin and its consequences, not only for yourself but also for those around you. Embrace personal responsibility for your actions and choices, striving to live with integrity. Prioritize honesty and truthfulness in all your relationships and dealings, rejecting deceit and dishonesty. Seek forgiveness and repentance when you fall short, knowing that God's mercy is always available. Use your influence to promote righteousness within your family and community, setting a positive example for others. Create a home environment where God's principles are honored and respected. Live with integrity, ensuring that your actions align with your beliefs and values.

Cultivating a Life of Prayer

Cleansing God, who removes sin and iniquity from our midst, I desire for Your truth and righteousness. Help me to understand the weight of my choices and the importance of living with integrity. Guide me in seeking forgiveness when I stumble, and empower me to use my influence for good. May my home be a place where Your truth is honored and Your presence is felt. Lead me in paths of righteousness, that my life may reflect Your holiness. In Jesus' name, Amen.

Week 39: Malachi - The Covenant of Marriage: Divorce and Faithfulness

Meet: The Women of Judah, Seeking Hope in Broken Covenants

Malachi, the last prophet of the Old Testament, delivers a message of rebuke and restoration to the people of Judah, addressing their spiritual apathy and unfaithfulness. Among his concerns is the prevalence of divorce and the disregard for the sanctity of marriage, a reflection of the declining moral state of the community. His words highlight the importance of honoring God's covenant, particularly within the context of marriage.

Malachi's message speaks directly to the pain and confusion that often accompany broken covenants, particularly for women who find themselves marginalized or abandoned. His words challenge men to honor their wives and to uphold the sacred bond of marriage while also encouraging women to seek solace and strength in God's unwavering love and justice.

Lessons Learned

1. The Sanctity of Marriage:
   - Malachi 2:14-16 emphasizes that God hates divorce, illustrating the sacredness of marriage and the importance of honoring the covenant commitment. It reminds women of the value and dignity of marriage in God's eyes.

2. God's Desire for Faithfulness:
   - Malachi 2:10-11 rebukes the people for their unfaithfulness, both to God and to their spouses. It highlights the importance of remaining faithful to our commitments.

3. The Impact of Divorce:
   - Malachi's words address the pain and suffering that divorce brings, particularly for women and children who are often left vulnerable and marginalized. It encourages sensitivity and support for those who have experienced divorce.

4. The Importance of Seeking God:
   - Malachi's call to repentance (Malachi 3:7) encourages women to turn to God in the midst of their pain and to seek His guidance and comfort.

5. The Promise of Blessing:
   - Despite the rebuke, Malachi also offers hope for restoration and blessing for those who return to God (Malachi 3:10-12). It reminds women that God's faithfulness endures, even when human commitments fail.

6. The Call to Justice:
   - Malachi 3:5 condemns those who exploit and mistreat others, including women. It challenges women to stand up for justice and to advocate for the rights of those who are vulnerable.

7. The Role of Prayer:
   - Malachi's message is infused with a sense of urgency and a call to pray for God's intervention. It encourages women to seek God's guidance and intervention through prayer.

8. The Importance of Community:
   - The communal nature of Malachi's message, addressed to the entire nation of Israel, highlights the importance of supporting and encouraging one another within the community of faith.

9. Hope for the Future:
   - Malachi's prophecy about the coming of the Messiah (Malachi 4:2) offers a glimpse of hope for a future marked by

healing and restoration. It reminds women that God's plan is ultimately one of redemption and renewal.

Finding Your Place

Embrace the sanctity of marriage, recognizing it as a sacred covenant before God. Commit to faithfulness in your relationships, striving to honor your commitments. Offer support and compassion to those who have experienced the pain of divorce, understanding the need for healing and restoration. Seek God's guidance and comfort through prayer, allowing His presence to bring solace during times of hardship. Advocate for justice and stand up against exploitation and abuse, recognizing the dignity of all individuals. Trust in God's promises of blessing and restoration, seeking to align your life with His will. Find strength and encouragement in your faith community, supporting and uplifting one another. Hold onto hope for the future, believing in God's plan for redemption and the coming of the Messiah.

Cultivating a Life of Prayer

Faithful God, who establishes, honors and renews covenants, thank You for Your commitment to restore and to redeem. Help me to understand the sanctity of marriage and to value its importance in Your eyes. Guide me in being faithful to my commitments, and grant me compassion for those who are hurting. Strengthen me to stand up for justice and to advocate for the vulnerable. Fill my heart with hope for Your promises, trusting in Your plan for the future. May my life reflect Your love and faithfulness, inspiring others to seek You. In Jesus' name, Amen.

Week 40: Matthew - Women in the Genealogy of Jesus

Meet: The Women of Jesus' Lineage, Threads of Faith and Redemption

The Gospel of Matthew, a powerful testament to Jesus Christ as the Messiah, opens with a genealogy that traces His lineage back to Abraham. While the focus of the genealogy is on tracing the line of kings and patriarchs, it includes four remarkable women: Tamar, Rahab, Ruth, and Bathsheba. These women, each with their own unique stories and challenges, stand out as essential threads in the tapestry of Jesus' lineage, demonstrating God's redemptive power and His choice to work through unconventional individuals.

The inclusion of these women, often overlooked or marginalized in societal norms, highlights the inclusive nature of God's plan and emphasizes that His salvation extends to all, regardless of their background or circumstances.

Lessons Learned

1. The Significance of Lineage:

   - Matthew 1:1-17 emphasizes the importance of tracing Jesus' lineage, reminding women that God works through generations to fulfill His promises.

2. God's Grace in Unconventional Stories:

   - The inclusion of Tamar, Rahab, Ruth, and Bathsheba (Matthew 1:3 6) demonstrates that God works through diverse circumstances and unconventional characters to bring about His plan.

3. The Power of Perseverance:
   - Tamar's story (Genesis 38) highlights her determination and courage to pursue justice and fulfillment, even when facing social stigma and adversity.

4. Redemption from the Past:
   - Rahab's transformation from a harlot to a woman of faith (Joshua 2, 6) illustrates the transformative power of God's grace, offering redemption from past mistakes and a new identity in Christ.

5. Faithfulness in Adversity:
   - Ruth's unwavering loyalty to Naomi and her trust in God (Ruth 1-4) showcase the strength of faith in challenging circumstances, inspiring women to remain steadfast even when facing difficulties.

6. The Impact of God's Mercy:
   - The inclusion of Bathsheba (2 Samuel 11-12) despite her involvement in David's sin, reminds women that God's mercy can extend to even those who have made mistakes.

7. The Importance of Legacy:
   - The presence of these women in Jesus' lineage emphasizes the lasting impact of their lives and the significance of leaving a legacy of faith and hope.

8. Breaking Down Societal Barriers:
   - The inclusion of these women, who often faced social stigma or challenging circumstances, demonstrates that God transcends societal limitations and values every individual.

9. The Inclusive Nature of God's Love:
   - The genealogy of Jesus highlights God's love and grace extended to all, regardless of background, demonstrating that redemption and salvation are available to everyone.

Finding Your Place

Recognize that God works through diverse circumstances and individuals to accomplish His purposes, finding hope even in unexpected stories. Embrace the transformative power of God's grace, believing in the possibility of redemption and a new identity in Christ. Hold onto your faith through difficult times, drawing strength from the examples of those who remained steadfast. Understand that God's mercy is available to all, and that He can redeem even those who have made mistakes. Value the lasting impact of your life and the legacy you leave behind. Remember that God embraces individuals from every background, recognizing the worth and dignity of all people. Embrace the universality of God's love, knowing that His grace extends to all.

Cultivating a Life of Prayer

Redemptive God, who weaves grace into our family histories, thank You for women who reminds us of Your power to redeem and restore. Help me to embrace Your grace, knowing that You offer transformation and a new identity in Christ. Strengthen me to stand firm in my faith and to trust in Your promises, even when facing challenges. Remind me of the impact of my life and the legacy I leave behind. May I live with an understanding of Your love that extends to all people, reflecting Your grace in my actions and choices. In Jesus' name, Amen.

Week 41: Mark - The Woman with the Issue of Blood

Meet: The Woman With Faith in Touch

The story of the woman with the issue of blood, as told in the Gospel of Mark, is a powerful testament to the transformative power of faith. Though unnamed, this woman suffers from a condition that has left her physically and socially ostracized. Driven by desperation and a deep faith in Jesus, she defies societal norms, pushing her way through a crowd and touching Jesus' garment, believing that this act will bring healing.

Her story highlights the importance of faith, the power of a single act of obedience, and the boundless compassion of Jesus. It speaks to the hearts of women who face physical and emotional struggles, reminding them that they can find healing and hope in Jesus.

Lessons Learned

1. The Importance of Perseverance:
   - The woman's determination to reach Jesus (Mark 5:25-28) demonstrates the importance of perseverance in pursuing healing and hope, even when facing obstacles.

2. Faith in Action:
   - The woman's act of touching Jesus' garment (Mark 5:28) shows that faith is not passive but actively seeks God's intervention.

3. God's Compassion for the Suffering:
   - Jesus' response to the woman (Mark 5:30-34) highlights His compassionate nature and His willingness to heal those who are in need.

4. Overcoming Social Barriers:

- The woman's courage to step out of the shadows (Mark 5:25-28) and to reach out to Jesus, despite societal expectations, encourages women to overcome social barriers in pursuing their faith.

5. The Power of Touch:

- The simple act of touching Jesus' garment (Mark 5:28) becomes a catalyst for healing. It reminds women that even small acts of faith can have significant consequences.

6. The Reality of Healing and Restoration:

- The woman's healing (Mark 5:29-34) illustrates the transformative power of faith and the reality of physical and emotional restoration in Christ.

7. The Importance of Identity:

- The woman's recognition that she has been healed (Mark 5:34) signifies the importance of understanding and embracing your own identity and the power that comes from recognizing God's work in your life.

8. The Significance of Faithfulness:

- The woman's unwavering faith and courage to act demonstrate the importance of faithfulness in pursuing God's promises.

9. The Role of Discipleship:

- The woman's desire to follow Jesus (Mark 5:34) reminds us that faith often leads to deeper connection with Christ and to actively living out one's belief.

Finding Your Place

Embrace perseverance in your faith journey, overcoming obstacles and distractions as you seek God's presence and guidance. Act upon your faith, taking steps to connect with Jesus and seeking His healing and power. Recognize your worth, regardless of societal limitations, and find courage to step out of your comfort zone in pursuit of a deeper relationship with God. Believe that Jesus is attentive to your needs and desires, trusting in His compassionate response to your prayers. Embrace the transformative power of faith, believing that God can bring about physical and emotional healing. Acknowledge the impact of God's work in your life, understanding your own identity in Him.   Be faithful in your commitment to Christ, allowing your life to be shaped by your beliefs. Strive to follow Jesus actively, embodying His teachings and sharing His message with others.

Cultivating a Life of Prayer

Compassionate Healing Savior, who restores and makes whole, inspire me to demonstrate unwavering faith in Your healing power. Help me to persevere in my pursuit of You, overcoming any obstacles that stand in my way. Teach me to actively express my faith through bold steps of obedience. Remind me of Your compassionate heart, and that You are always listening to my prayers. Empower me to experience Your transformative healing in my life and to live out my faith in all that I do. Help me to recognize my identity in You and to follow Your leading with joy and dedication. In Jesus' name, Amen.

Week 42: Luke - Mary, the Mother of Jesus

Meet: Mary, the Woman of Humble Obedience

Mary, a young woman from Nazareth, is chosen by God for a monumental task: to be the mother of Jesus. The Gospel of Luke beautifully portrays Mary's journey, highlighting her faith, humility, and unwavering obedience to God's will. When the angel Gabriel visits Mary with the news that she will conceive and give birth to the Son of God, she responds with a simple yet profound declaration, "I am the Lord's servant. May your word to me be fulfilled" (Luke 1:38).

Mary's story is a testament to the transformative power of saying "yes" to God. Her willingness to embrace the unexpected and to surrender her own plans to God's purpose serves as an inspiring example for women of all ages.

Lessons Learned

1. Humility in the Face of God's Calling:

   - Mary's humble acceptance of God's plan (Luke 1:38) demonstrates the importance of recognizing our position before God and responding with a willingness to serve His purposes.

2. Trusting in God's Promises:

   - Despite the challenges and uncertainties that accompany her pregnancy, Mary trusts in God's promise (Luke 1:38) and faithfully awaits the fulfillment of His word.

3. Finding Strength in God:

- Mary's song of praise, the Magnificat (Luke 1:46-55), reveals her deep faith and reliance on God's strength, even in the midst of significant changes and challenges.

4. Embracing the Unexpected:

- Mary's journey highlights the unexpected turns that life can take and the importance of being open to God's leading, even when it deviates from our own plans.

5. The Power of Obedience:

- Mary's "yes" to God (Luke 1:38) is a powerful act of obedience, demonstrating that saying yes to God often requires courage and a willingness to step outside our comfort zones.

6. The Beauty of Surrender:

- Mary's surrender to God's will, relinquishing control over her future, exemplifies the beauty of allowing God to work in and through our lives.

7. The Joy of Motherhood:

- Mary's experience of motherhood (Luke 2:7) celebrates the sacred bond between a mother and child and the joy that comes from nurturing and raising children.

8. The Importance of Community:

- Mary's visit to Elizabeth (Luke 1:39-45) and her presence among the disciples (Acts 1:14) highlight the importance of community and support in navigating life's journey.

9. The Legacy of Faith:

- Mary's unwavering faith in God and her role as the mother of Jesus leave a lasting legacy of devotion and obedience, inspiring generations to come.

Finding Your Place

Cultivate a spirit of humility, recognizing your need for God's guidance and acknowledging His sovereignty. Place your trust in God's promises, believing in His faithfulness to fulfill His word. Find strength in God during times of uncertainty and change, relying on His power to sustain you. Embrace the unexpected turns in your life, seeking God's purpose in every situation. Respond to God's call with obedience, even when it requires courage to step outside your comfort zone. Surrender your plans to God's will, trusting in His ability to work through you. Celebrate the joy and beauty of motherhood, nurturing and caring for children as a sacred gift. Seek support and encouragement from your community of faith, building relationships that strengthen and uplift you. Live a life of faith and obedience, leaving a legacy that inspires others to follow God.

Cultivating a Life of Prayer

Blessed Lord, who honors and uses humble servants for Your work, grow my faith and obedience in You everyday. Help me to cultivate a heart of humility, recognizing Your sovereignty in my life. Strengthen my trust in Your promises, and guide me to find strength and hope in You. May I embrace the unexpected turns in my life, seeking Your purpose in every situation. Empower me to respond to Your call with courage and obedience, surrendering my plans to Your perfect will. Help me to cultivate a life of prayer and to find joy in serving You. Surround me with a supportive community of believers, and may my life reflect a legacy of faith and devotion. In Jesus' name, Amen.

Week 43: John - Mary Magdalene

Meet: Mary Magdalene, the Woman of Deep Devotion

Mary Magdalene, a prominent figure in the Gospel of John, is remembered as a woman of deep faith and unwavering devotion to Jesus. Known for her passionate love for Jesus and her unwavering commitment to Him, Mary Magdalene stands out as a powerful example of faithful discipleship. She is present at the foot of the cross as Jesus is crucified, witnesses His burial, and is the first person to see Him after His resurrection.

Mary Magdalene's journey through sorrow and grief, culminating in the joy of encountering the risen Christ, offers a powerful testament to the transformative power of faith and the enduring nature of love. Her story inspires women to seek a deep and personal relationship with Jesus, to remain steadfast in their faith even through suffering, and to embrace the joy that comes from encountering the risen Lord.

Lessons Learned

1. The Depth of Faith and Love:
   - Mary Magdalene's presence at the foot of the cross (John 19:25) and at the tomb (John 20:1) illustrates the depth of her love and devotion to Jesus. It encourages women to cultivate a deep and personal relationship with Christ.

2. The Power of Witnessing the Resurrection:
   - Mary Magdalene is the first person to witness the risen Christ (John 20:14-18). This experience emphasizes the transformative power of encountering the resurrected Christ, reminding women of the hope and assurance found in His victory over death.

3. The Importance of Prayer and Perseverance:
   - Mary Magdalene's persistence in seeking Jesus, going to the tomb early in the morning (John 20:1), shows the importance of prayer and perseverance in our faith journeys.

4. Overcoming Grief and Sorrow:
   - Mary Magdalene's transition from grief and despair (John 20:11-13) to joy and hope (John 20:16-18) exemplifies the healing and transformation that come through faith in Christ.

5. The Call to Share the Good News:
   - Mary Magdalene becomes the first messenger of the resurrection, sharing the good news with the disciples (John 20:18). It reminds women of the importance of sharing the Gospel and of proclaiming the message of hope.

6. The Importance of Recognizing Jesus:
   - Mary Magdalene initially mistakes Jesus for the gardener (John 20:14-15), highlighting the importance of recognizing Jesus in unexpected ways and allowing Him to transform our perceptions.

7. The Strength of Women in Faith:
   - Mary Magdalene's story demonstrates the strength and devotion of women who stand by Jesus through adversity and who embrace the hope of His resurrection.

8. The Role of Women in the Early Church:
   - Mary Magdalene is a prominent figure in the early church, highlighting the vital role women played in sharing the Gospel and in building the community.

9. The Joy of Encountering the Risen Christ:
   - Mary Magdalene's experience of encountering the risen Christ highlights the joy and transformation that come from a personal relationship with Jesus.

Finding Your Place

Cultivate a deep and personal relationship with Jesus, allowing your love for Him to guide your choices and actions. Embrace the hope and assurance found in Christ's resurrection, believing in His victory over death. Be persistent in seeking God's presence through prayer and spiritual disciplines. Allow Jesus to heal your grief and sorrow, transforming your pain into hope. Share the Gospel message boldly, becoming a messenger of Christ's love and redemption. Open your heart to recognize Jesus in unexpected ways and allow Him to transform your perceptions. Find strength and encouragement in your faith, knowing that God empowers you to overcome challenges. Engage actively in the community of believers, sharing the joy of faith and contributing to the growth of the church. Experience the transformative joy that comes from a personal encounter with Jesus.

Cultivating a Life of Prayer

Risen Savior, who reveals Yourself to those who seek You, You are the source of life and hope. Help me to deepen my relationship with You, and to experience the joy of Your presence. Guide me through times of grief and loss, and allow me to be a messenger of Your resurrection. Strengthen my faith in You and empower me to share Your love and hope with others. May my life reflect the transformation You bring, and may I find joy in my journey of faith. In Your name, Amen.

Week 44: Acts - Lydia, the Businesswoman

Meet: Lydia, the Woman of Hospitality and Faith

Lydia, a successful businesswoman from Thyatira, is introduced in the book of Acts as a woman of influence and faith. Her story unfolds in Philippi, where she encounters the Apostle Paul and his companions during their missionary journey. Known for her trade in purple cloth, a symbol of wealth and status, Lydia is also a devout worshiper of God.

The narrative highlights her openness to the Gospel message, her immediate baptism, and her generous hospitality in opening her home to Paul and his companions. Lydia's story demonstrates that faith can flourish in the midst of a busy life and that God can use individuals from all walks of life to advance His Kingdom.

Lessons Learned

1. Openness to the Gospel:
   - Lydia's attentiveness to Paul's message (Acts 16:14) highlights the importance of being open to God's Word and allowing it to transform our hearts.

2. The Importance of Baptism:
   - Lydia's baptism, along with her household (Acts 16:15), signifies the commitment to following Jesus and becoming a part of the Christian community.

3. Hospitality and Service:

- Lydia's generosity in opening her home to Paul and his companions (Acts 16:15) demonstrates the importance of hospitality and using one's resources to serve others.

4. The Impact of a Woman of Influence:

- Lydia's role as a successful businesswoman and her influence within the community illustrate the potential for women to impact their surroundings for Christ.

5. The Integration of Faith and Work:

- Lydia's story shows that faith is not separate from our daily lives but should permeate every aspect, including our work and businesses.

6. The Power of Personal Testimony:

- Lydia's conversion and subsequent baptism likely influenced others in her community, highlighting the impact of personal testimonies in spreading the faith.

7. The Role of Women in the Early Church:

- Lydia's home becomes a Meeting place for the believers (Acts 16:40), emphasizing the significant role women played in the growth and establishment of the early church.

8. The Value of Community:

- The fellowship established in Lydia's home demonstrates the importance of Christian community, offering support and encouragement to one another.

9. The Joy of a Transformed Life:

- Lydia's conversion and her commitment to Christ bring a new dimension of joy and purpose to her life. It encourages women to seek the fulfillment found in a relationship with God.

Finding Your Place

Be open to hearing the Gospel message, allowing God's Word to challenge and transform your life. Commit to following Jesus Christ through baptism, joining the community of believers. Extend hospitality and generosity to others, using your resources and talents to serve your community. Embrace the influence God has given you in your sphere of work and relationships, reflecting Christ in all you do. Integrate your faith into every aspect of your life, recognizing that your work and your faith are interconnected. Share your personal testimony of faith, inspiring others through your experiences with God's grace. Support the work of your church and community, creating welcoming spaces for fellowship and worship. Embrace the joy that comes from a transformed life, sharing that joy with others.

Cultivating a Life of Prayer

Provider God, who blesses and uses our skills for Your kingdom, who also calls us to service, open my heart to receive Your Word, and help me to share my faith with courage and generosity. May I use my influence to build Your kingdom, and create welcoming spaces for others to experience Your love. Grant me the joy of a transformed life and the desire to share that joy with my community. In Jesus' name, Amen.

Week 45: Romans - Junia: Women in Apostleship

Meet: Junia, an Early Apostle

Junia, a woman whose name appears in the book of Romans, is a significant figure who challenges traditional interpretations of leadership within the early church. Paul, in his letter to the Romans, describes Junia as an "apostle" (Romans 16:7), a title usually associated with men in the New Testament.

Junia's presence and ministry, along with the recognition she receives from Paul, highlight the potential for women to serve in leadership roles within the church. Her story sparks crucial conversations about the role of women in ministry and challenges traditional interpretations that have limited women's participation in leadership and service.

Lessons Learned

1. The Role of Women in Apostleship:
   - The mention of Junia as an apostle (Romans 16:7) challenges traditional interpretations of leadership and affirms that women, too, can be called to serve as apostles, carrying the message of the Gospel and building up the church.

2. The Importance of Recognizing God's Call:
   - Junia's ministry as an apostle demonstrates that God calls individuals to unique roles and responsibilities, regardless of gender, challenging us to recognize and affirm the gifts and calling of all believers.

3. The Value of Diversity in Leadership:
   - The presence of Junia as an apostle highlights the importance of diverse voices and perspectives within the

church, reminding us that God uses individuals from all walks of life to advance His kingdom.

4. The Strength of Women in Ministry:
   - Junia's ministry as an apostle inspires women to embrace their calling and to use their gifts and talents to serve God and others.

5. Embracing the Inclusive Nature of the Gospel:
   - The recognition of Junia as an apostle reminds us that the Gospel is for all people, regardless of gender, and that God calls everyone to serve Him in various ways.

6. The Importance of Scriptural Interpretation:
   - The debate surrounding Junia's role highlights the importance of carefully interpreting Scripture, recognizing that traditional interpretations may need to be challenged and reframed in light of new perspectives.

7. The Need for Openness to God's Calling:
   - Junia's story encourages women to be open to God's calling and to embrace the opportunities He presents, even when those opportunities challenge societal norms.

8. The Power of Faithful Witness:
   - Junia's ministry as an apostle serves as a reminder of the transformative power of faithful witness and the importance of sharing the Gospel message.

9. The Legacy of Women in Ministry:
   - Junia's story leaves a legacy of courage and faith for women in ministry, inspiring them to embrace their calling and to use their gifts to advance God's kingdom.

Finding Your Place

Recognize that women are called to serve in various roles within the church, including positions of leadership. Be open to God's calling on your life, embracing the opportunities He presents, even when they challenge societal norms. Embrace the diversity of gifts and talents within the church, recognizing the value of all voices and perspectives. Use your unique skills and passions to serve God and others. Seek to understand Scripture with a heart open to new perspectives and interpretations. Be a bold witness for the Gospel, sharing your faith with courage and conviction. Remember the legacy of women in ministry, drawing inspiration from their courage and faithfulness.

Cultivating a Life of Prayer

Welcoming God, who acknowledges and values every contribution, You call us to serve You, regardless of gender or background. Help me to recognize and embrace the gifts and calling You have placed on my life. Guide me to use my talents to build Your kingdom and to stand with other women who are called to ministry. Empower me to interpret Your word with discernment and to share Your message with boldness. May my life be a testament to Your love and grace as I strive to live a life that honors You. In Jesus' name, Amen.

Week 46: 1 Corinthians - Chloe: House Churches and Women's Leadership

Meet: Chloe, A Leader in the Early Church

Chloe, a woman mentioned in Paul's first letter to the Corinthians, is a significant figure in the early church. Though little is known about her personal life, Chloe's name appears in connection with the Corinthians church (1 Corinthians 1:11), suggesting she was a prominent and influential member. She is associated with the concept of "house churches," where early believers often gathered for fellowship, worship, and teaching within homes.

While Chloe herself is not explicitly described as a leader, her connection to the church at Corinth, and the mention of her "people" (1 Corinthians 1:11), suggest a leadership role. This connection highlights the importance of women in early Christian communities, particularly in the context of house churches, where women often played vital roles in hosting gatherings, offering hospitality, and contributing to spiritual instruction.

Lessons Learned

1. The Significance of House Churches:

   - The mention of Chloe and her "people" (1 Corinthians 1:11) underscores the importance of house churches in the early church, suggesting that women played significant roles in hosting and nurturing Christian communities.

2. Women's Leadership in the Early Church:

   - Chloe's association with the Corinthian church, likely acting as a host for a house church, demonstrates the significant leadership roles women played in the early church, challenging traditional interpretations that limit women's participation in ministry.

3. The Impact of Hospitality:
   - Chloe's role as a host emphasizes the importance of hospitality in building and strengthening community. It teaches women to open their homes and lives to others, creating spaces for fellowship and spiritual growth.

4. The Power of Influence:
   - Chloe's influence within the Corinthian church, as evidenced by Paul's reference to her "people," highlights the significant influence women can have within their communities.

5. The Importance of Unity:
   - Paul's letter to the Corinthians, addressing divisions within the church (1 Corinthians 1:10-12), emphasizes the need for unity and cooperation among believers, reminding women of the strength found in a united church.

6. The Importance of Discernment:
   - Paul's letter highlights the need for discernment in discerning truth from error (1 Corinthians 2:14). It encourages women to carefully evaluate teachings and to remain grounded in the truth of Scripture.

7. The Value of Spiritual Gifts:
   - The diversity of spiritual gifts within the church (1 Corinthians 12:7-11) reminds women that God gives unique gifts to each person. It encourages them to embrace and use their gifts for the benefit of the community.

8. The Importance of Love:
   - Paul's emphasis on love as the greatest expression of faith (1 Corinthians 13:1-13) inspires women to prioritize love in all

their relationships, recognizing it as the foundation of a strong community.

9. The Strength of a Woman's Witness:
   - Chloe's presence within the church at Corinth, her influence, and her hospitality, suggest that women played vital roles in the spread of the Gospel, reminding us that women's testimonies are essential to the growth and development of the faith.

Finding Your Place

Embrace the importance of hospitality, creating spaces for fellowship and spiritual growth within your home and community. Recognize and celebrate the leadership roles women played in the early church, and champion their continued contribution to the church today. Use your influence to bring unity and peace to your community. Cultivate discernment, ensuring that your faith is grounded in biblical truth. Embrace the unique gifts God has given you, using them to serve and to build up the church. Let love be the foundation of all your relationships, reflecting Christ's love in your actions. Remember the power of a woman's testimony, sharing your faith with boldness and conviction.

Cultivating a Life of Prayer

Lord of the Church, You have called us to be one body, united in Your love. Help me to embrace the importance of hospitality and to create welcoming spaces within my community. Guide me to use my gifts and talents to serve You, and to recognize the valuable contributions of women in the church. Fill my heart with Your love, and inspire me to build bridges of unity and understanding. May my life be a testament to Your truth and a reflection of Your grace, as I strive to share Your message with others. In Jesus' name, Amen.

Week 47: 2 Corinthians - Daughters of God: Embracing Divine Adoption

Meet: The Daughters of God, Redeemed and Beloved

In his second letter to the Corinthians, the Apostle Paul addresses the challenges and misunderstandings that arose within the church. This letter serves to defend his authority as an apostle while also emphasizing themes of reconciliation, grace, and the transformative power of the Gospel.

While the letter focuses primarily on Paul's ministry and his relationship with the Corinthians, it implicitly speaks to the experiences of women within the early church. Paul's message of reconciliation and his affirmation of the new life found in Christ offer profound encouragement and assurance for women who may be struggling with feelings of inadequacy, exclusion, or a lack of belonging.

Lessons Learned

1. The Transforming Power of the Gospel:
   - 2 Corinthians 5:17 highlights the new creation that occurs in Christ. It encourages women to embrace the transformative power of the Gospel, recognizing that they are made new in Christ, regardless of their past.

2. The Gift of Adoption:
   - 2 Corinthians 6:18 emphasizes that God offers adoption as children of God. This reminds women that they are not merely servants but beloved children, cherished and accepted by God.

3. The Importance of Reconciliation:
   - Paul's call for reconciliation (2 Corinthians 5:18-20) encourages women to pursue peace and restoration in their

relationships, reflecting the reconciliation God offers through Christ.

4. The Strength of God's Comfort:
   - 2 Corinthians 1:3-4 emphasizes that God is our source of comfort. This reminds women that they are never alone in their struggles and that God's comfort is always available.

5. The Role of Intercession:
   - Paul's prayer for the Corinthians (2 Corinthians 1:11) highlights the importance of prayer in supporting and advocating for others.

6. The Call to Live Worthy of the Calling:
   - The challenge to live worthy of the calling (2 Corinthians 5:20) encourages women to strive for a life that reflects their new identity in Christ.

7. The Importance of Integrity:
   - Paul's defense of his ministry and character (2 Corinthians 1:12-14) underscores the importance of integrity in leadership, reminding women to live with honesty and authenticity.

8. The Power of Generosity:
   - 2 Corinthians 9:6-7 emphasizes cheerful giving, challenging women to practice generosity and to share their resources with others.

9. The Impact of Faithfulness:
   - Paul's unwavering commitment to serving the Corinthians, even through difficult times, inspires women to remain faithful in their calling and to persevere in their service to God.

Finding Your Place

Embrace the transformative power of the Gospel, recognizing the new life you have in Christ and the freedom it brings. Trust in God's love and acceptance, understanding that you are His beloved child. Seek reconciliation with others, fostering peace and unity in your relationships. Draw strength from God's comfort, knowing that He is with you in every circumstance. Pray for others, supporting and advocating for their needs. Strive to live a life that reflects your new identity, allowing God's grace to shape your actions and choices. Uphold integrity in your life, reflecting honesty and authenticity. Practice generosity, sharing your resources and talents with others. Be inspired by Paul's unwavering faithfulness, committing to serve God with dedication and perseverance.

Cultivating a Life of Prayer

God of grace and love, thank You for the gift of adoption as Your children. Help me to embrace my new identity in You and to live in the freedom and love that You offer. Guide me to seek reconciliation and to extend Your grace to others. Fill me with Your comfort, reminding me of Your constant presence in my life. Teach me to pray for others, and to be a faithful and dedicated servant in Your kingdom. May my life reflect Your love and truth as I strive to live a life that honors You. In Jesus' name, Amen.

Week 48: Galatians - Women's Freedom in Christ

Meet: The Women of Galatia, Embracing Liberation

The book of Galatians, written by the Apostle Paul, addresses a critical issue facing the early church: the danger of legalism and the distortion of the true message of salvation. Paul passionately defends the freedom that comes through faith in Jesus Christ, challenging those who would add requirements of the Jewish law to the Gospel message.

While not explicitly addressing women's roles, Galatians' central theme of freedom resonates deeply with women who have faced limitations and restrictions based on their gender. The concept of living by faith, not by works of the law, offers a powerful message of liberation, emphasizing that women, like all believers, are freed from the burdens of legalistic expectations and empowered to live in the grace and truth of Christ.

Lessons Learned

1. The Power of Grace:
   - Galatians 2:16 emphasizes that we are justified by faith, not by works of the law. This reminds women that their worth and acceptance before God come through His grace, not through their own efforts or societal expectations.

2. The Freedom Found in Christ:
   - Galatians 5:1 calls believers to stand firm in the freedom that Christ provides. It encourages women to embrace the liberty that comes from a relationship with Christ, breaking free from any legalistic or restrictive traditions.

3. Living by the Spirit:

- Galatians 5:16-25 describes the fruits of the Spirit, emphasizing the importance of living according to the Spirit's guidance, rather than being bound by laws or external regulations.

4. The Importance of Unity:

- Galatians 3:28-29 highlights that there is no longer Jew or Gentile, slave or free, male or female, for we are all one in Christ. It emphasizes the unity and equality that Christ brings to all believers.

5. The Call to Serve Others:

- Galatians 5:13-14 encourages believers to serve one another in love, reminding women that their faith is expressed through acts of kindness and generosity.

6. The Danger of Legalism:

- Paul's strong condemnation of legalism (Galatians 4:21-31) warns against returning to a mindset that emphasizes external rules and rituals over the grace and freedom found in Christ.

7. The Promise of Spiritual Growth:

- The fruits of the Spirit (Galatians 5:22-23) highlight the potential for spiritual growth and transformation when believers allow the Holy Spirit to guide their lives.

8. The Power of Faith in Action:

- The call to live by faith (Galatians 2:20) reminds women that faith is not just a belief system but a way of life, actively expressing their commitment to God through their actions.

9. The Role of Women in God's Kingdom:

- While not explicitly stated, the message of Galatians challenges women to fully embrace their place within God's kingdom, free from the limitations of societal norms and expectations.

Finding Your Place

Embrace the freedom that comes through faith in Jesus Christ, recognizing that your worth and acceptance before God are based on His grace, not your own efforts. Reject any legalistic traditions or expectations that limit your spiritual growth and freedom. Allow the Holy Spirit to guide your life, fostering the fruits of the Spirit in your actions and decisions. Celebrate the unity and equality that Christ brings to all believers, recognizing your place within God's family. Commit to serving others with love and generosity, expressing your faith through acts of kindness. Strive to live out your faith actively, letting your life be a reflection of Christ's love and truth. Remember that you are empowered by God's grace to live a life of freedom and purpose.

Cultivating a Life of Prayer

Liberating Savior, who sets us free from all bondage, help me to embrace the freedom You offer through faith in Jesus Christ. Guide me to live by Your Spirit, rejecting any legalistic restrictions and embracing the transformative power of Your grace. Fill me with a deep appreciation for the unity and equality You have brought to all believers. Empower me to serve others with love and to live out my faith with integrity and joy. May my life be a testament to Your liberating power and to the freedom found in Your love. In Jesus' name, Amen.

Week 49: Ephesians - The Bride of Christ: Corporate Identity in the Church

Meet: The Church, a Bride Adorned for Christ

The book of Ephesians, one of Paul's most profound and expansive letters, focuses on the unity and purpose of the Church, as the body of Christ. The letter, addressed to believers in Ephesus, emphasizes the importance of understanding their shared identity in Christ, their calling to unity and holiness, and their role in furthering God's mission.

Paul's powerful imagery of the church as the bride of Christ (Ephesians 5:25-32) reminds believers of the deep and enduring relationship they share with Jesus, a relationship marked by love, unity, and submission. This imagery challenges women to embrace their unique role within the church, recognizing their individual and collective beauty and significance in God's plan.

Lessons Learned

1. The Unity of the Church:
   - Ephesians 4:4-6 emphasizes that there is one body and one Spirit, encouraging women to recognize the importance of unity and cooperation within the church.

2. The Bride of Christ:
   - Ephesians 5:25-32 uses the imagery of the church as the bride of Christ, underscoring the deep and enduring love that exists between Christ and His followers.

3. The Call to Holiness:
   - Ephesians 4:1-3 calls for a life of holiness, reminding women to strive for personal growth and transformation that reflects Christ's character.

4. The Strength of Submission:
   - Ephesians 5:22-24 describes a woman's submission to her husband, not as a sign of inferiority, but as a reflection of the church's submission to Christ.

5. The Role of Mutual Submission:
   - Ephesians 5:21 emphasizes that husbands should submit to their wives as Christ submitted to the Father, advocating for a reciprocal respect and submission within marriage.

6. The Importance of Love and Respect:
   - Ephesians 5:25-33 calls for husbands to love their wives as Christ loved the church. It teaches women to expect love and respect within marriage.

7. The Power of God's Word:
   - Ephesians 6:17 underscores the importance of the Word of God in equipping believers for spiritual battles. It encourages women to engage with scripture and to allow its truths to guide their lives.

8. Living as Ambassadors for Christ:
   - Ephesians 4:1-3 challenges believers to live a life worthy of their calling, reminding women that their actions should reflect their commitment to Christ.

9. The Joy of a Transformed Life:
   - Ephesians 1:3-14 celebrates the spiritual blessings available to those who belong to Christ. It encourages women to embrace the joy and peace that come from being united with Christ.

Finding Your Place

Embrace the unity of the Church, recognizing that you are part of a larger body of believers. Cherish your relationship with Christ, understanding the depth of His love for you. Strive for personal holiness, allowing the Spirit to guide and transform your life. Embrace a spirit of mutual submission within your marriage, honoring and respecting both your husband and God. Expect to be loved and respected in your relationship, valuing the principles of Christ's love. Let the Word of God be a source of guidance and strength in your life. Live in a way that reflects your commitment to Christ, showcasing your faith through your actions. Embrace the joy and peace that come from being united with Christ, celebrating the blessings of your new life in Him.

Cultivating a Life of Prayer

God of love and unity, teach me to embrace the unity of the Church and to cherish my relationship with You. Guide me in seeking holiness and in living a life worthy of Your calling. Teach me to cultivate mutual submission and respect in my relationships, reflecting the love of Christ. Strengthen my faith through Your Word and fill me with the joy of being united with You. May my life reflect Your love and grace as I strive to be a part of Your kingdom. In Jesus' name, Amen.

Week 50: Philippians - Motherhood of Timothy: Impact of Godly Parenting

Meet: Lois and Eunice, Shaping a Young Leader

The story of Timothy, a young disciple of Paul, reveals the powerful impact of godly parenting on shaping the life of a future leader. While Paul is famously credited with mentoring Timothy, the influence of his mother, Eunice, and his grandmother, Lois, cannot be overlooked. These women are described as having instilled a deep faith in Timothy from a young age, laying a foundation for his later dedication to ministry and service.

The story of Timothy and his family underscores the importance of parental influence in nurturing spiritual growth and leadership. It highlights how the faithfulness of mothers, grandmothers, and other significant women can shape a child's faith journey and contribute to the development of future generations of believers.

Lessons Learned

1. The Legacy of Faith:
   - Timothy's faith, passed down through his mother Eunice and grandmother Lois (2 Timothy 1:5), demonstrates the power of a mother's faith in shaping her children's spiritual lives.

2. The Importance of Early Nurture:
   - Timothy's early instruction in Scripture (2 Timothy 3:15) shows the importance of introducing children to God's word at a young age, laying a foundation for their faith.

3. The Power of a Mother's Influence:
   - The influence of Eunice and Lois on Timothy highlights the significant role mothers play in shaping the faith and character of their children.

4. The Impact of Intergenerational Faith:
   - The passing of faith from grandmother to mother to son exemplifies the importance of intergenerational spiritual connection and the enduring influence of faith.

5. The Courage to Embrace Calling:
   - Despite his youth, Timothy embraces his leadership role (1 Timothy 4:12) due to the strong foundation of faith provided by his mother and grandmother.

6. The Importance of Modeling Faithfulness:
   - The story of Eunice and Lois encourages women to live out their faith consistently, setting an example of dedication to God for their children.

7. The Role of Prayer in Nurturing Faith:
   - The example of Eunice and Lois likely includes a commitment to prayer for Timothy, highlighting the importance of prayer for children and their spiritual development.

8. The Joy of Spiritual Inheritance:
   - The passing down of faith through generations demonstrates the joy and privilege of sharing God's love and truth with those we love.

9. The Value of Multi-Generational Support:
   - Timothy's story encourages women to seek support and encouragement from other women in their families and communities, creating a network of faith and guidance.

Finding Your Place

Recognize the powerful impact you have on your children and grandchildren as a mother, grandmother, or mentor, allowing your faith to shape their lives. Embrace the importance of introducing children to God's Word early in their lives, laying a foundation for their spiritual growth. Live a life of faith that reflects your devotion to God, serving as a positive example for those you love. Pray for your children and grandchildren, seeking God's blessing and guidance for their journeys. Encourage the next generation to embrace their God-given calling and to serve Him with their unique gifts. Celebrate the joy of intergenerational faith, finding strength and unity in your connection with family and other women who share your beliefs.

Cultivating a Life of Prayer

Faithful God, who works through generations, thank You for the role of mothers in our spritual walk who nurture our faith from a young age until spritual maturity. Grant me also the wisdom and guidance to nurture my children and grandchildren in Your ways. Fill me with a passion to share Your Word with them and to live a life that reflects Your love and faithfulness. Strengthen me to pray for their spiritual development, and to encourage them to embrace the callings You have placed on their lives. Help us to build a legacy of faith that spans generations and glorifies Your name. In Jesus' name, Amen.

Week 51: Colossians - Instructions for Women About Christian Living

Meet: The Women of Colossae, Embracing God's Truth

The letter to the Colossians, written by the Apostle Paul, addresses a community grappling with false teachings and the allure of worldly philosophies. Paul emphasizes the supremacy of Christ, reminding believers of their identity and purpose in Him. While the letter broadly addresses the entire community, it implicitly speaks to the specific needs and challenges faced by women in their daily lives.

Paul's teachings on submission, gentleness, and the importance of living with wisdom and grace offer guidance for women seeking to navigate the complexities of their roles within the church and society. They provide a framework for understanding their position as believers and their call to live out their faith in a way that reflects God's love and truth.

Lessons Learned

1. The Supremacy of Christ:

   - Colossians 1:15-18 emphasizes the centrality of Christ, reminding women that He is the head of all creation and the source of all truth and wisdom.

2. Living in the Light of Christ:

   - Colossians 3:1-4 challenges believers to seek what is above, prioritizing spiritual values over worldly desires. It encourages women to seek God's direction and to allow His truth to guide their lives.

3. The Importance of Humility and Gentleness:
   - Colossians 3:12-13 instructs believers to be compassionate, kind, humble, gentle, and patient. It emphasizes the importance of developing these qualities in all our interactions.

4. The Role of Wives and Husbands:
   - Colossians 3:18-19 discusses the roles of wives and husbands in marriage. It reminds women of their call to respect and submit to their husbands, while also highlighting the husband's responsibility to love his wife unconditionally.

5. The Value of Prayer:
   - Colossians 4:2 encourages believers to persevere in prayer. It reminds women of the importance of seeking God's guidance and strength through prayer, both individually and collectively.

6. The Strength of the Word:
   - Colossians 3:16 emphasizes the importance of letting the word of Christ dwell richly within us. It encourages women to engage with Scripture, allowing God's truth to shape their thoughts and actions.

7. Embracing God's Will:
   - Colossians 1:9-10 reminds believers to walk in a manner worthy of God. It challenges women to align their lives with God's will and to seek to please Him in all they do.

8. The Power of Forgiveness:
   - Colossians 3:13 encourages believers to forgive one another, reflecting God's forgiveness. It reminds women to extend grace and to seek reconciliation in their relationships.

9. The Joy of a Transformed Life:
   - Colossians 3:15-17 celebrates the joy of finding peace and unity in Christ. It encourages women to seek the peace and contentment that come from a relationship with Christ.

Finding Your Place

Center your life on Christ, recognizing His supremacy and seeking to align your life with His teachings. Prioritize spiritual values, allowing God's truth to shape your desires and actions. Cultivate humility, gentleness, and patience in your interactions with others. Embrace a spirit of mutual submission and respect within your marriage, honoring the principles of Christ's love. Engage in prayer, seeking God's guidance and strength in all you do. Let God's Word be a source of wisdom and encouragement for your life. Strive to live a life that is worthy of your calling in Christ, reflecting His love and grace in all you do. Extend forgiveness to those who have wronged you, seeking reconciliation and peace. Find joy and contentment in your relationship with Christ, allowing His presence to fill your life.

Cultivating a Life of Prayer

Transformative Lord, who guides us in living out our faith daily, inspire me to center my life on Christ, recognizing His supremacy and seeking to live according to His teachings. Guide me in cultivating humility and gentleness in my interactions with others. Teach me to embrace mutual submission and respect within my marriage, reflecting the love of Christ. Strengthen my faith through Your Word and empower me to live a life that is pleasing to You. May I extend forgiveness to those who have wronged me, seeking reconciliation and peace. Fill me with the joy of Your presence and the assurance of Your love. In Jesus' name, Amen.

Week 52: 1 & 2 Thessalonians - The Second Coming of Christ

Meet: The Thessalonians, Living in Hopeful Anticipation

The Thessalonians, recipients of Paul's letters to the Thessalonians, were a vibrant community of early Christians facing challenges and persecution. Paul's letters provide guidance, encouragement, and instruction as they navigate their newfound faith.

The Thessalonians' strong eschatological focus, their concern with the end times and Jesus' second coming, shapes much of Paul's teaching. He commends their commitment to faith, love, and hope, while also addressing misunderstandings and encouraging moral purity and diligence. The Thessalonians serve as an inspiring example of how to live with an awareness of Christ's imminent return and how to maintain steadfastness under pressure.

Lessons Learned

1. The Importance of Hope:

   - 1 Thessalonians 1:10 shows how the Thessalonians' hope in Jesus' return spurred them to action. It teaches young people that their hope in Christ's second coming should motivate them to live righteously.

2. The Promise of Christ's Return:

   - 1 Thessalonians 4:16-17 describes the return of Christ with a shout. It reminds young people that Jesus's return is a future event to be eagerly anticipated and prepared for.

3. The Power of Faith and Love:
   - The Thessalonians are commended for their work of faith, labor of love, and steadfastness of hope (1 Thessalonians 1:3). It underscores the importance of these virtues in the Christian life.

4. Living in Light of Christ's Return:
   - 1 Thessalonians 5:6 encourages believers to be alert and prepared for Christ's coming. It challenges young people to live with an awareness of the end times and to be ready for Jesus' return.

5. The Importance of Spiritual Growth:
   - 2 Thessalonians 1:3 commends the Thessalonians for their growing faith and love. It encourages young people to seek continual spiritual development.

6. The Necessity of Self-Control:
   - 1 Thessalonians 5:6-8 calls for spiritual sobriety and self-control. It reminds young people to maintain a disciplined and focused lifestyle, preparing themselves for Christ's return.

7. Understanding Sound Doctrine:
   - Paul addresses misconceptions about the Day of the Lord (2 Thessalonians 2:1-2) highlighting the importance of accurate teaching and understanding in matters of faith.

8. The Role of Prayer in Ministry:
   - Paul's requests for prayer (2 Thessalonians 3:1-2) emphasizes the vital role of prayer in supporting the spread of the Gospel and overcoming challenges.

9. The Importance of Perseverance:
   - Paul's encouragement to the Thessalonians to remain steadfast in their faith (2 Thessalonians 3:13) teaches young people the significance of enduring through trials and remaining faithful to their beliefs.

Finding Your Place

Let the hope of Christ's return influence your daily actions and attitudes, motivating you to live righteously. Embrace the principles of faith, love, and hope as the foundation of your Christian walk. Stay alert and prepared for Jesus' return, keeping your life focused and ready for His coming. Seek continual spiritual growth, striving to deepen your relationship with Christ. Maintain self-control, recognizing the importance of a disciplined and focused lifestyle. Seek sound teaching and understanding of God's Word, particularly in regards to His return. Engage in prayer, both for yourself and for the spread of the Gospel. Persevere in your faith journey, remaining steadfast even when faced with difficulties.

Cultivating a Life of Prayer

Hopeful Lord, who assures us of Your return and eternal promise, fill me with hope for Your coming, and guide me to live a life that reflects that hope in my actions and choices. Strengthen my faith, love, and hope, reminding me of the importance of these virtues in my walk with You. Help me to remain vigilant and prepared for Your return, living a life that is focused and ready. Empower me to seek spiritual growth continually, and teach me to live with self-control and discipline. Guide me in understanding Your Word, especially in regards to the events surrounding Your return. May my prayers be a source of support and strength for myself and others as we await Your glorious coming. In Jesus' name, Amen.

BONUS WEEKS

Week 53: 1 Timothy - Widows in the Early Church: Care and Ministry

Meet: The Widows of Ephesus, Finding Support and Purpose

In his first letter to Timothy, Paul addresses practical matters concerning the organization and leadership of the church in Ephesus. Within this context, he provides specific instructions regarding the care and support of widows within the community. This section highlights the importance of caring for the vulnerable, particularly widows, who often faced significant social and economic challenges in the ancient world.

Paul's instructions regarding widows reveal the early church's commitment to providing both material and spiritual support to those in need. It also addresses the role of widows in ministry, recognizing their potential to contribute to the life of the church. This passage encourages women to embrace compassion and to actively participate in caring for the vulnerable within their communities.

Lessons Learned

1. The Church's Responsibility to Widows:
   - 1 Timothy 5:3-16 outlines the church's responsibility to care for widows, particularly those who are truly in need. It teaches young women the importance of compassion and the community's role in providing support.

2. Honoring Widows:
   - 1 Timothy 5:3 encourages honoring widows who are truly widows. It emphasizes the respect and dignity due to older women who have lost their husbands.

3. The Importance of Family Support:

   - 1 Timothy 5:4, 8, 16 highlights the role of family members in caring for widows. It reminds young people of their responsibilities to their own families.

4. The Role of Widows in Ministry:

   - 1 Timothy 5:9-10 outlines qualifications for widows who desire to be enrolled for ministry in the church. It acknowledges the valuable contributions that widows can make to the community.

5. The Dangers of Idleness:

   - 1 Timothy 5:13 warns against idleness among younger widows. It encourages young women to be active and productive members of their community.

6. The Value of Good Works:

   - The qualifications for widows enrolled for ministry (1 Timothy 5:10) emphasize the importance of a life marked by good works and service to others.

7. Discernment in Providing Support:

   - The distinction between true widows and those who have family support (1 Timothy 5:3-16) teaches the importance of discernment in offering support, ensuring that resources are directed to those truly in need.

8. The Importance of Leadership:

   - Paul's instructions to Timothy about caring for widows highlight the role of leadership in addressing the needs of the community.

9. The Church as a Family:

   - The care for widows within the church reflects the concept of the church as a family, where members are responsible for one another's well-being.

Finding Your Place

Embrace the call to compassion, actively seeking ways to support and care for the vulnerable in your community. Recognize the importance of honoring older women and those who have experienced loss, treating them with respect and dignity. Fulfill your responsibilities towards your family members, offering support and care as needed. If you are a widow, consider the opportunities for ministry within your church, using your gifts and experience to serve others. Live a life that is marked by good works and service, reflecting your faith through action. Practice discernment in offering support to others, ensuring that your resources are used wisely. Support those in leadership positions as they seek to address the needs of the community. Contribute to building a church community that embodies the love and care of a family.

Cultivating a Life of Prayer

Compassionate God, who cares for the vulnerable, guide me to continue caring for those needing such. Help me to embrace compassion and to actively seek ways to support those in need within my community. Teach me to honor older women and to recognize their value and contributions. Guide me in fulfilling my responsibilities towards my family, offering support and care. May my life be marked by good works and service, reflecting Your love for others. Grant me discernment in offering aid, ensuring that my resources are used wisely. In Jesus' name, Amen.

Week 54: 2 Timothy - Lois and Eunice: Intergenerational Faith Transmission

Meet: Lois and Eunice, the Women of Faith

Lois and Eunice, grandmother and mother to the young pastor Timothy, emerge as influential figures in the book of 2 Timothy. Though they are not directly mentioned in the book's events, their impact on Timothy's life is acknowledged by Paul, who credits them with nurturing his faith from an early age.

This story, while focusing on Paul's mentoring of Timothy, underscores the power of intergenerational faith, highlighting the significant role mothers and grandmothers play in passing down faith and values to future generations. The example of Eunice and Lois provides a powerful model for women seeking to influence the faith journeys of their children and grandchildren.

Lessons Learned

1. The Legacy of Faith:
   - The mention of Eunice and Lois (2 Timothy 1:5) as Timothy's mentors emphasizes the importance of passing faith down through generations, recognizing the enduring influence of family on spiritual formation.

2. The Impact of Mothers and Grandmothers:
   - The influence of these women on Timothy's life shows the powerful impact that mothers and grandmothers can have on their children's faith. It encourages women to embrace their role in nurturing future generations.

3. The Power of Early Instruction:
   - Timothy's early instruction in Scripture (2 Timothy 3:15) underlines the importance of introducing children to God's word from an early age, laying a strong foundation for their faith.

4. The Value of Spiritual Mentorship:
   - The story of Eunice and Lois, teaching Timothy about God's Word, highlights the significant role of mentorship and guidance in faith development. It encourages women to seek mentors for themselves and to guide others in their faith.

5. The Importance of Living Out One's Faith:
   - The faith of Eunice and Lois likely involved not just words but also living out their faith consistently, serving as powerful role models for their children and grandchildren.

6. The Importance of Prayer:
   - The influence of Eunice and Lois on Timothy likely included consistent prayer for him, demonstrating the power of prayer for children and their spiritual growth.

7. Faith as a Family Legacy:
   - Timothy's story illustrates how faith can be passed down through generations, creating a strong spiritual lineage.

8. Building a Community of Faith:
   - The example of Eunice and Lois encourages women to create and support communities that nurture faith, encouraging and supporting one another in their journeys.

9. The Power of Example:
   - The actions of Eunice and Lois serve as a powerful reminder that a mother's example and influence can profoundly shape the lives of her children.

Finding Your Place

Embrace your role as a mother, grandmother, or mentor in shaping the faith of those around you. Prioritize introducing children to God's Word, laying a strong foundation for their spiritual journey. Live out your faith consistently, serving as a positive role model for your family. Invest in prayer for your children and grandchildren, seeking God's guidance and protection for their lives. Seek mentors for your own growth and consider becoming a mentor to others. Celebrate the joy of sharing your faith with your family and building a legacy of faith across generations. Participate in and support faith communities, fostering a network of support and encouragement for women in their journeys.

Cultivating a Life of Prayer

Equipping God, who provides wisdom and strength for leadership, guide me as I seek to teach others whether my children, friends, neighbour or just brethens about Your love and truth. Help me to live a life that reflects Your Word and that inspires them to follow You. Strengthen me in prayer for their spiritual growth, and may my influence help them grow in their faith. May our family be a testament to the enduring power of a legacy of faith. In Jesus' name, Amen.

Week 55: Titus - Older Women as Mentors

Meet: Older Women, Guides in the Faith

The book of Titus, one of the Pastoral Epistles written by the Apostle Paul, provides guidance for Titus, a young leader tasked with establishing and strengthening the church on the island of Crete. Paul's instructions to Titus address specific issues within the church, including the importance of sound doctrine, ethical conduct, and leadership.

Within this context, Paul highlights the vital role of older women in mentoring and teaching younger women, reminding them to embrace their experiences and wisdom to guide the next generation. Titus's story emphasizes the value of intergenerational relationships within the church and the power of older women to shape the spiritual growth of younger women.

Lessons Learned

1. The Value of Older Women's Wisdom:
   - Titus 2:3-5 emphasizes the role of older women in teaching and mentoring younger women. It highlights the importance of valuing the wisdom and experience of older generations.

2. The Importance of Sound Teaching:
   - Titus 2:1 underscores the need for sound doctrine and emphasizes the importance of teaching truth and encouraging spiritual growth.

3. The Power of Example:
   - Older women are encouraged to be examples of godliness and to live lives that reflect their faith (Titus 2:3-5). This

emphasizes the importance of living out one's faith and serving as a positive influence.

4. The Role of Mentorship:
   - The instruction for older women to teach and guide younger women (Titus 2:3-5) highlights the importance of mentorship in nurturing and developing faith.

5. The Strength of a Woman's Voice:
   - The call for older women to teach others (Titus 2:3-5) challenges the traditional limitations on women's roles and affirms the value of their voices in shaping spiritual understanding.

6. The Importance of Integrity:
   - The emphasis on integrity and holiness (Titus 2:3-5) reminds women that their actions and choices should reflect the truth of the Gospel.

7. The Power of Grace:
   - Titus 2:11-14 speaks of the transformative power of God's grace. This encourages women to rely on God's grace for strength and guidance in living out their faith.

8. Building a Strong Community:
   - The emphasis on nurturing younger women within the community (Titus 2:3-5) highlights the importance of building a strong and supportive faith community.

9. The Legacy of Faith:
   - The call to mentor and to teach younger women (Titus 2:3-5) encourages women to consider the lasting impact of their influence and to leave a legacy of faith.

Finding Your Place

Value the wisdom and experience of older women, seeking their guidance and mentorship in your faith journey. Embrace the importance of sound doctrine, seeking to understand and live according to God's truth. Strive to live a life that reflects your faith, serving as a positive example for others. Recognize the significance of mentorship, both as a mentor and as a mentee, in fostering spiritual growth. Use your voice to teach and to guide others, encouraging their faith and understanding. Maintain integrity in your actions and choices, ensuring your life reflects the teachings of Christ. Rely on God's grace for strength and transformation as you navigate the journey of faith. Contribute to building a strong and supportive faith community. Consider the legacy you are leaving behind and how you can positively influence future generations.

Cultivating a Life of Prayer

Heavenly Father, who guides and empowers, inspire me to recognize and value the wisdom and experience of those who have gone before me, seeking their guidance in my own journey. Grant me the strength to live a life that reflects Your truth, and to use my knowledge to mentor and guide others. May I be a faithful witness to Your grace and a source of encouragement to those around me. Inspire me to build strong and supportive faith communities that offer guidance and support for women of all ages. May my life be a legacy of faith that inspires future generations to follow You. In Jesus' name, Amen.

Week 56: Philemon - Apphia: Women in Church Leadership

Meet: Apphia, Co-Leader in the Colossian Church

The letter to Philemon, a personal appeal from the Apostle Paul regarding a runaway slave named Onesimus, offers a brief but significant glimpse into the life of Apphia, a woman who appears to hold a leadership position within the church in Colossae. Paul addresses the letter to Philemon, Apphia, and Archippus, "our fellow worker," indicating a shared ministry and responsibility within the church.

While little is known about Apphia's specific role, the fact that she is addressed alongside Philemon suggests a position of authority and influence within the church. Her presence challenges traditional interpretations of women's roles in the early church, highlighting the inclusion of women in leadership and decision-making.

Lessons Learned

1. Women in Leadership:

   - Paul's address to Apphia (Philemon 1:2) suggests that she held a prominent role in the Colossian church. This affirms the active participation and leadership of women in the early church.

2. Shared Ministry:

   - The letter being addressed to Philemon, Apphia, and Archippus (Philemon 1:1-2) suggests a collaborative leadership model, where men and women worked together to guide and nurture the community.

3. The Value of Partnership:
   - Paul's acknowledgment of their shared ministry (Philemon 1:1) emphasizes the importance of partnerships and collaborative efforts in advancing the work of the church.

4. Hospitality and Church Life:
   - The gathering of the church in Philemon's house (Philemon 1:2) implies that Apphia likely played a role in hosting and providing hospitality for the community.

5. The Importance of Discernment:
   - The context of the letter, dealing with the sensitive issue of a runaway slave, suggests that Apphia would have been involved in decision-making and discernment related to church matters.

6. The Power of Influence:
   - Apphia's influence within the church is evident from Paul's direct appeal to her regarding Onesimus, suggesting that her opinion and decision carried weight within the community.

7. The Call to Unity:
   - The letter to Philemon emphasizes the importance of unity and reconciliation within the church, encouraging believers to work together toward a common purpose.

8. The Role of Women in Reconciliation:
   - Apphia's likely role in facilitating the reconciliation between Philemon and Onesimus highlights the significant role women played in promoting peace and unity.

9. Leaving a Legacy of Service:
   - Though little is known about Apphia, her inclusion in Paul's letter suggests a lasting legacy of service and leadership within the Colossian church, inspiring women to embrace their call to ministry.

Finding Your Place

Embrace your calling to serve in leadership roles within your church, recognizing that God gifts women with the ability and authority to lead. Seek opportunities to partner with others in ministry, collaborating to build and strengthen the church. Extend hospitality and create welcoming spaces for your community, fostering fellowship and spiritual growth. Exercise discernment in church matters, seeking God's wisdom and contributing to decision-making processes. Use your influence to promote unity and reconciliation, advocating for justice and peace within your community. Be inspired by the example of women like Apphia, whose faithfulness and leadership contributed to the growth of the early church.

Cultivating a Life of Prayer

God of unity and strength, thank You for the example of Apphia and her leadership in the Colossian church. Help me to embrace my calling to serve and to work collaboratively with others in building Your kingdom. Guide me in using my influence for good, promoting unity, reconciliation, and justice within my community. May my life be a reflection of Your love and grace as I seek to serve Your purposes. In Jesus' name, Amen.

Week 57: Hebrews - Women of Faith

Meet: The Unnamed Women of Faith, Heroes in the Shadows

The book of Hebrews, a powerful exposition of the supremacy of Christ and the new covenant, includes a remarkable chapter dedicated to celebrating the faith of those who came before. Hebrews 11, often referred to as the "Hall of Faith," lists a series of biblical figures who demonstrated extraordinary faith in God, serving as examples for believers of all generations.

While the chapter primarily highlights the accomplishments of men like Abraham, Moses, and David, it also acknowledges the contributions of women whose names are not explicitly mentioned. This inclusion, though subtle, emphasizes that women have always played a vital role in God's story, exhibiting unwavering faith, courage, and resilience.

Lessons Learned

1. The Universality of Faith:

- The inclusion of unnamed women in the "Hall of Faith" (Hebrews 11:35) highlights that faith is not limited to gender or social status. It teaches women that they are called to live by faith, just as men are.

2. The Strength of Women in the Face of Adversity:

- The reference to women who received back their dead (Hebrews 11:35) points to the resilience and strength of women in facing challenging circumstances, trusting in God's power even in the face of death.

3. Faithfulness in the Midst of Persecution:

   - Hebrews 11:35 mentions those who were tortured, refusing to be released. This reminds women that standing firm in faith often involves facing persecution and hardship.

4. The Importance of Trusting God's Promises:

   - The examples of faith throughout the chapter demonstrate the power of trusting in God's promises, even when they seem impossible or delayed.

5. The Role of Women in God's Plan:

   - The inclusion of women in the "Hall of Faith" underscores their vital role in God's plan, demonstrating that their faithfulness contributes to the unfolding of His purposes.

6. The Legacy of Faithfulness:

   - The stories of these women, though unnamed, inspire future generations to live by faith, leaving a legacy that encourages others to trust in God.

7. The Power of Unseen Faith:

   - Many of the women mentioned in Hebrews 11 acted on faith without seeing the immediate results. It teaches women to trust in God's power, even when His plans are not fully revealed.

8. The Importance of Perseverance:

   - The examples of faith in Hebrews 11 often involve enduring hardship and challenges. It encourages women to persevere in their faith, knowing that God is with them.

9. The Inspiration of Community:

   - The collective witness of the "Hall of Faith" reminds women that they are part of a larger community of believers, encouraging them to support and inspire one another in their faith journeys.

Finding Your Place

Embrace your calling to live by faith, knowing that God values your faithfulness and your contributions to His kingdom. Draw strength from the examples of women who have faced adversity and remained steadfast in their trust in God. Remember that you are not alone in your faith journey, and find encouragement in the community of believers who have gone before you and those who stand beside you today. Trust in God's promises, even when they seem impossible or delayed, knowing that He is faithful to fulfill His word. Be prepared to face challenges and persecution, holding onto your convictions with courage and determination. Live a life that reflects your faith, inspiring others to seek God's truth and embrace His promises. Leave a legacy of faithfulness for future generations, knowing that your actions and choices can impact the world around you.

Cultivating a Life of Prayer

God of faithfulness, thank You for the women of faith whose stories, life and testimonies inspire us. Strengthen my faith, that I may persevere through challenges and trust in Your promises. May I find courage and strength in the examples of those who have gone before me, and may my life reflect the unwavering faith that You desire. Guide me to be a part of a community that supports and encourages one another in our faith journeys. In Jesus' name, Amen.

Week 58: James – Women's Faith and Works

Meet: Women of Faith, Trusting in Action

The book of James, known for its emphasis on the harmony between faith and action, offers a powerful message about living out one's faith through tangible deeds. James addresses believers who were scattered, reminding them that faith without works is dead, and that faith should be demonstrated through consistent, purposeful actions.

In this spirit, women who await God's promises can find encouragement in James's words, embracing the call to live out their trust in God through their actions, even as they wait on Him to fulfill His promises. James's letter particularly connects with women who struggle to balance faith with action in their various roles. His practical wisdom offers guidance for women wrestling with how to demonstrate their faith while facing life's challenges, whether in the workplace, home, or church community.

Lessons Learned

1. The Importance of Faith in Action:

- James 2:14-26 states, "faith by itself, if it is not accompanied by action, is dead." This powerful declaration teaches women that true faith is more than just belief; it is actively demonstrated through good works and compassionate service.

2. The Power of Words:

- James 3:1-12 emphasizes the importance of controlling the tongue, reminding women that their words have the power to build up or tear down.

3. The Call to Impartiality:

   - James 2:1-9 condemns showing favoritism in the congregation, teaching women to treat all individuals with equal respect, compassion, and love.

4. The Importance of Caring for Others:

   - James 1:27 defines true religion as caring for orphans and widows. This challenges women to engage in acts of social justice, advocating for the vulnerable and marginalized.

5. The Value of Humility:

   - James 4:6-10 encourages women to submit to God and to resist pride. It reminds them that true humility is essential for spiritual growth and for honoring God.

6. The Strength of Patience:

   - James 5:7-8 calls for patience in waiting for the Lord's return. It teaches women to cultivate perseverance, trusting in God's timing and plan.

7. The Power of Prayer:

   - James 5:16-18 emphasizes the effectiveness of fervent prayer. It encourages women to engage in prayer as a powerful force for change and transformation.

8. The Importance of Spiritual Growth:

   - James 1:2-4 encourages women to view trials as opportunities for spiritual growth and to persevere through hardship, trusting in God's strengthening power.

9. Steadfastness as a Testimony of Faith:

   - James 5:10-11 highlights the perseverance of prophets who awaited God's promises. Women can find inspiration in their endurance, viewing steadfastness as a powerful testimony of unwavering faith.

Finding Your Place

Let your faith be demonstrated through your actions, actively engaging in good works and compassionate service. Guard your speech, using your words to build up and encourage others. Treat all individuals with equal respect and compassion, showing no favoritism. Actively participate in social justice efforts, caring for the vulnerable and marginalized. Cultivate humility in your interactions and decisions, recognizing God's sovereignty and authority. Embrace patience and perseverance as you navigate life's challenges, trusting in God's timing and plans. Engage in fervent prayer, seeking God's guidance and intervention. Strive for spiritual growth, allowing God to shape and transform you. Live a life of faithfulness and purpose, leaving a legacy of love and service to the world.

Cultivating a Life of Prayer

God of Action, who calls us to live out our faith, encourage me to demonstrate my faith through my actions and to use my words to build up others. Guide me to treat all people with respect and love, showing no favoritism. Inspire me to care for those in need and to advocate for justice in my community. Strengthen me to persevere through trials, and to seek Your wisdom in all my decisions. Empower me to live with integrity, aligning my actions with my beliefs. Teach me to trust in the power of prayer, and to maintain humility in my relationship with You. May my life be a testament to the transformative power of genuine faith. In Jesus' name, Amen.

Week 59: 1 & 2 Peter - Women Living as God's Chosen People

Meet: The Women of God, A Chosen People

Peter, one of Jesus' closest disciples, plays a pivotal role in the early church, and his letters offer guidance and encouragement to believers facing various challenges. The epistles of First and Second Peter address Christians who are scattered throughout the world, enduring persecution and navigating a society that often seeks to undermine their faith.

Peter's letters emphasize the importance of living in accordance with God's will and purpose, reminding believers of their identity as chosen people and challenging them to maintain faithfulness through trials. These letters offer a powerful message of hope, assuring believers that they are not alone and that God's power will sustain them in their journey.

Lessons Learned

1. The Importance of God's Choosing:

   - 1 Peter 2:9 reminds believers that they are "a chosen people, a royal priesthood, a holy nation, God's own people." This reinforces women's worth and identity as chosen by God, despite societal limitations.

2. The Strength of Holy Living:

   - 1 Peter 1:15-16 encourages believers to live holy lives, setting a standard for behavior and conduct that reflects the righteousness of God. This challenges women to live lives of integrity and purpose.

3. The Role of Suffering:
   - 1 Peter 3:14-17 speaks about enduring persecution for righteousness, reminding women that suffering for their faith is not a cause for shame but a testament to their faithfulness.

4. The Importance of Submissive Faith:
   - 1 Peter 2:18-25 reminds believers to submit to authority for the sake of Christ. It encourages women to view submission as an act of faith and obedience to God, even when facing difficult circumstances.

5. The Power of Prayer:
   - 1 Peter 3:12 emphasizes the power of prayer. It encourages women to turn to prayer as a source of strength, comfort, and guidance during times of need.

6. The Promise of Eternal Glory:
   - 1 Peter 1:4-9 describes the inheritance believers have in Christ, reminding women of the hope for eternal life and the future glory that awaits them.

7. The Importance of Unity:
   - 1 Peter 3:8-9 encourages unity and harmony within the community of believers, highlighting the strength found in supporting and loving one another.

8. The Value of Humility:
   - 1 Peter 5:5-6 reminds women that true leadership is characterized by humility, challenging those in positions of authority to serve with integrity.

9. Standing Firm in Truth:
   - 2 Peter 2:1-3 warns believers about false teachers and encourages discernment in adhering to the truth of the Gospel, reminding women to be discerning in their beliefs and choices.

Finding Your Place

Embrace your identity as a chosen child of God, understanding the unique purpose He has for your life. Live a life that reflects God's holiness, striving to honor Him in your actions and thoughts. Trust in God's power to sustain you through persecution and to bring about justice. Embrace a spirit of submission to authority, knowing that it is an act of faith and obedience to God. Turn to prayer as a source of strength and comfort, seeking God's guidance during times of need. Hold fast to the hope of eternal life, allowing it to shape your choices and actions. Foster unity within your community, offering support and encouragement to other believers. Seek humility in your interactions with others, recognizing the importance of servant leadership. Guard yourself against false teachings, remaining steadfast in your belief in the truth of the Gospel.

Cultivating a Life of Prayer

Faithful God, thank You for reminding us that we are Your chosen people. Help me to embrace my identity as a daughter of God and to live a life that honors Your will. Strengthen me to endure persecution with grace, and to submit to authority with a spirit of obedience. Grant me the strength of prayer, and fill me with hope for the eternal glory that awaits me. Guide me in fostering unity and supporting my community, and may I be a discerning follower of Your truth. In Jesus' name, Amen.

Week 60: 1, 2 & 3 John - Walking in the Light

Meet: John, the Beloved Disciple, Champion of Truth and Love

John, the apostle and beloved disciple of Jesus, is known for his deep love and understanding of Jesus Christ. He pens the Gospel of John, as well as three epistles that offer profound insights into the nature of God, the importance of walking in truth, and the significance of love as the defining characteristic of a Christian life.

John's letters, addressed to believers facing various challenges, address themes of fellowship, discernment, and the assurance of salvation. His words serve as a powerful guide for navigating the complexities of faith and for maintaining a relationship with God that is grounded in truth and love.

Lessons Learned

1. The Importance of Living in Truth:
   - 1 John 1:6-7 emphasizes that "if we claim to have fellowship with Him and yet walk in the darkness, we lie and do not live out the truth." This reminds women that true faith is not just about belief but also about living consistently with God's word.

2. The Source of True Love:
   - 1 John 4:7-8 teaches that "love is from God." This underscores that love is not merely an emotion but a divine characteristic that should permeate our lives.

3. The Relationship Between Love and Obedience:
   - 1 John 2:3-6 states, "We know that we have come to know him if we keep his commands." It highlights the connection between love for God and obedience to His will.

4. The Power of Fellowship:
   - 1 John 1:7 encourages believers to walk in the light and have fellowship with one another. This emphasizes the importance of building strong and supportive relationships within the Christian community.

5. Discerning Truth from Error:
   - 1 John 4:1-3 encourages testing spirits to discern truth. This reminds women to be careful in their pursuit of knowledge, ensuring that they are following teachings that align with God's Word.

6. The Assurance of Salvation:
   - 1 John 5:13 provides confidence in eternal life through faith in Jesus. It reassures women that their faith in Christ brings them eternal security.

7. The Evidence of Love:
   - 1 John 3:14 emphasizes that love for one another is evidence of true faith. It challenges women to actively demonstrate their love for others through their actions.

8. The Role of the Holy Spirit:
   - 1 John 4:13 reminds believers that God's Spirit dwells within them. This encourages women to rely on the Spirit's guidance and power in their lives.

9. Walking in the Light:
   - John's repeated emphasis on walking in the light (1 John 1:7) encourages women to align their lives with God's truth and to live in a way that reflects His character.

Finding Your Place

Embrace the truth of God's Word, allowing it to shape your thoughts, actions, and relationships. Cultivate a life rooted in love, reflecting God's love for you and for others in all your interactions. Seek to live in obedience to God's commands, recognizing that true love is expressed through action. Build strong and supportive relationships within your faith community, finding strength and encouragement in fellowship with other believers. Be discerning in your pursuit of knowledge and teachings, ensuring that they align with the truth of the Gospel. Rest assured in the promise of eternal life through your faith in Christ. Demonstrate your faith through acts of love and service, extending compassion and kindness to others. Rely on the Holy Spirit to guide and empower you in your walk with God. Strive to live a life that reflects God's light and truth, allowing His love to shine through in all you do.

Cultivating a Life of Prayer

Loving God, who is the source of all truth and love, inspire me to embrace Your truth and to live a life that reflects Your love. Guide me to walk in the light, allowing Your Word to shape my choices and actions. Strengthen my commitment to loving others and to building a strong and supportive community of faith. Grant me discernment in my pursuit of knowledge and reassure me of the promise of eternal life through faith in Christ. May my life be a testament to Your love and a reflection of Your light. In Jesus' name, Amen.

Week 61: Jude - Tactics of the Adversary

Meet: Jude, the Defender of Truth

Jude, the brother of James and a servant of Jesus Christ, delivers a powerful message of warning and exhortation to believers who face the threat of false teachings and moral compromise. His short epistle, one of the most urgent and passionate in the New Testament, emphasizes the importance of contending for the faith, standing firm against those who seek to twist the Gospel and lead others astray.

Jude's words address the tactics of the adversary, drawing on biblical examples to illustrate the dangers of straying from God's truth and the importance of remaining grounded in faith. His message challenges believers to recognize and resist the subtle and insidious strategies used by the enemy to deceive and undermine their faith.

Lessons Learned

1. The Importance of Contending for the Faith:
   - Jude 1:3 urges believers to "contend for the faith." This reminds women that actively defending their beliefs is essential, particularly against the dangers of false teachings and compromise.

2. Recognizing the Enemy's Tactics:
   - Jude 1:4 warns of those who have secretly slipped in to distort the Gospel. It challenges women to be vigilant and discerning, recognizing the deceptive tactics used by those who seek to mislead others.

3. The Power of Deception:

- Jude 1:10-12 describes the deceptive tactics of the devil and his followers, reminding women to be cautious about those who promote teachings or practices that contradict the truth of the Gospel.

4. Remembering God's Judgment:

- Jude 1:5-7 recounts historical examples of God's judgment on those who disobeyed His commands. This serves as a powerful reminder of the consequences of turning away from God.

5. The Role of Humility and Respect:

- Jude 1:9 highlights the example of Michael the archangel, who, when contending with Satan, spoke with respect and reverence. It teaches women to approach disagreements with humility and grace, even when defending truth.

6. The Importance of Building Up in Faith:

- Jude 1:20-21 encourages believers to build themselves up in their faith. This reminds women to prioritize spiritual growth and to engage in prayer, study, and fellowship to strengthen their faith.

7. The Call for Mercy:

- Jude 1:22-23 calls for showing mercy to those who are struggling or doubting. It encourages women to approach others with compassion and understanding, seeking to guide them toward the truth.

8. Standing Firm in Unity:

- Jude 1:19 emphasizes the importance of unity and encouragement among believers, especially in the face of challenges.

9. Trusting in God's Protection:
   - Jude 1:24-25 assures believers that God will keep them from stumbling. It teaches women to trust in God's faithfulness and to rely on His strength during times of vulnerability.

Finding Your Place

Commit to actively contending for the truth of the Gospel, standing firm against any distortions of God's message. Develop discernment, recognizing false teachings and resisting those who seek to deceive you. Remember God's judgment on those who reject His truth, allowing this reminder to motivate you to live in obedience. Engage in disagreements with humility and respect, seeking to address conflict peacefully and effectively. Invest in building your faith through prayer, study, and fellowship with other believers. Extend mercy and compassion to those struggling with doubts, offering guidance and support. Strengthen your connection to other believers, fostering unity and encouragement within your faith community. Trust in God's protection and faithfulness, recognizing His role as your protector and guide.

Cultivating a Life of Prayer

God of truth and faithfulness, I want to be vigilant in guarding the truth of Your Word, and to recognize the deceptive tactics of the enemy. Strengthen my resolve to contend for the faith, standing firm against false teachings and compromises. Guide me in approaching disagreements with humility and respect, and in extending mercy to those who are struggling. May my life be marked by steadfast faith and a commitment to living in accordance with Your truth. Protect me from spiritual deception, and fill me with the assurance of Your faithfulness and love. In Jesus' name, Amen.

Week 62: Revelation - Women in the End Times

Meet: The Woman Clothed with the Sun, a Symbol of God's People

The book of Revelation, a complex and symbolic tapestry of visions and prophecies, offers a glimpse into the future, revealing God's ultimate plan for history. While the book is filled with dramatic imagery and often challenging interpretations, it ultimately points to a message of hope, the triumph of good over evil, and the establishment of a new heaven and a new earth.

One of the most prominent female figures in Revelation is the "woman clothed with the sun" (Revelation 12:1-6), often interpreted as representing God's people, both Israel and the Church. Her story, intertwined with the dragon (Satan) and the birth of a male child (Jesus), highlights the spiritual battles that believers face, the protection God provides, and the ultimate victory of Christ over evil.

Lessons Learned

1. The Reality of Spiritual Warfare:
   - The dragon's attempt to devour the child (Revelation 12:4) reveals the ongoing spiritual battle between good and evil. This teaches women to recognize the reality of spiritual warfare and the need for vigilance in their faith journey.

2. The Protection of God:
   - The woman is given wings to escape the dragon (Revelation 12:6, 14), symbolizing God's protection and provision for His people. It encourages women to trust in God's power to shelter and safeguard them.

3. The Perseverance of the Saints:

   - The woman's endurance in the wilderness (Revelation 12:6, 14) highlights the perseverance of God's people, even in the face of persecution and hardship.

4. The Victory of Christ:

   - The ultimate victory of the male child (Jesus) over the dragon (Revelation 12:7-12) assures believers that Christ will triumph over evil, bringing ultimate redemption.

5. The Importance of Remaining Faithful:

   - The dragon's pursuit of the woman (Revelation 12:13-17) emphasizes the need for believers to remain steadfast in their faith, even during times of intense opposition.

6. The Hope of a New Creation:

   - Revelation 21-22 describes a new heaven and a new earth where God dwells with His people. This provides a vision of hope for a future free from pain and suffering.

7. The Call to Witness:

   - The woman's role in bearing witness to the truth (Revelation 12:17) encourages women to boldly share their faith and to stand firm in their convictions.

8. The Strength of Community:

   - The imagery of the woman and her offspring representing God's people highlights the importance of community and support among believers.

9. The Importance of Spiritual Discernment:

   - The deceptive nature of the dragon (Revelation 12:9) reminds women of the need for spiritual discernment and vigilance in identifying false teachings and resisting evil influences.

Finding Your Place

Recognize the reality of spiritual warfare and prepare to stand firm in your faith. Trust in God's protection and provision, knowing that He will shield you from harm. Persevere through trials and challenges, drawing strength from God's faithfulness and the hope of ultimate victory. Embrace your role as a witness for Christ, sharing the Gospel boldly and defending the truth. Find support and encouragement within your faith community, recognizing the strength that comes from unity. Develop spiritual discernment, being vigilant in identifying false teachings and resisting the influence of evil. Hold onto the hope of a new creation, where God's presence will bring peace and healing.

Cultivating a Life of Prayer

Sovereign God, who reigns over all creation, thank You for the hope and assurance found in the book of Revelation. Help me to recognize the reality of spiritual warfare and to stand firm in my faith. Grant me Your protection and guide me through times of difficulty. Empower me to be a faithful witness to Your truth and to find strength in the community of believers. May I live with hope for the future, knowing that You are in control and that Your victory is assured. In Jesus' name, Amen.

Conclusion

As we reach the end of this study, we reflect on the lives, lessons, and legacies of the women we have encountered. Each chapter has introduced us to stories that span history, culture, and faith, yet their relevance remains timeless. We have seen these women face trials, make bold choices, endure suffering, and celebrate joy—all while remaining tethered to their faith in God. Through their examples, we have glimpsed what it means to live a life of purpose, resilience, and devotion.

These women teach us that a life of faith is not without challenges or failures. Each story offers a testament that God's purpose can shine through any circumstance, turning moments of weakness into testimonies of strength, and moments of loss into seasons of growth. Just as these women responded to God's call in their lives, we, too, are invited to live out our faith courageously, to trust in God's plan, and to walk in the path He has set before us.

Carrying the Lessons Forward

Throughout this study, we have sought to uncover more than historical details; we have searched for lessons that can transform us. These women embody traits like boldness, wisdom, compassion, humility, and resilience. They show us that even in the quiet, uncelebrated moments, God is at work. Their stories remind us to value the gifts we have, to cultivate courage in adversity, and to remain steadfast in our faith, no matter the circumstance.

As we leave behind the pages of these narratives, let's remember the teachings that have challenged and changed us. Just as Abigail's wisdom led her to defuse a volatile situation, we, too, can seek God's wisdom in times of conflict. Like Ruth, who found hope in the midst of loss, we can trust God to bring new life to our broken places. And as Mary, the mother of Jesus, faithfully followed God's call, we can also surrender to His will, knowing that He holds our future.

Finding Our Place in God's Grand Narrative

These women's stories are not only individual journeys but threads in the grand tapestry of God's narrative. They each played a role in a much larger story—a story that continues to unfold in our lives today. We are all called to take our place in this unfolding narrative, each with our unique roles, strengths, and experiences. God has not finished writing His story, and He invites each of us to be part of it.

As we reflect on the lives of these women, we see that God values every voice, every story, and every heart. You, too, are part of this divine tapestry. You are called to live out your faith boldly, to love deeply, to seek wisdom, and to embrace the role that God has prepared uniquely for you. Just as these women were shaped by their faith, we are called to let our faith shape us, allowing God's presence to guide us as we step into our future.

Living a Life of Prayer and Purpose

One of the most profound takeaways from our study is the power of prayer and its role in a life of faith. The women in these stories often turned to God in moments of need, frustration, celebration, and pain. They teach us that prayer is not only a tool for asking but a way of aligning our hearts with God's purposes. It's where we find strength, comfort, direction, and peace.

As you move forward from this study, let prayer be the foundation of your life. Let it be the first response to your joy, your worry, your dreams, and your doubts. Cultivate a heart that seeks God's will, that listens to His voice, and that is open to His leading. Through prayer, we find our true identity, our mission, and the strength to live a life that honors God, just as these women did.

A Lasting Legacy of Faith

In the end, the impact of each woman's life can be seen in the legacy she left behind—a legacy that endures through the pages of Scripture and in the lives of those inspired by her story. As we conclude this study, consider what legacy you will leave. How will your life reflect the love, courage, wisdom, and faith you have seen in these women? Will you, like them, pass down a heritage of faith to future generations, sharing with others the truths that have shaped your journey?

Your legacy may be one of quiet strength, resilient faith, or sacrificial love. Whatever it may be, remember that God can use your story just as He used theirs. You are called to a life of purpose and influence, one that will echo beyond your own lifetime. Just as these women's lives remind us of God's faithfulness, may your life be a reminder to others of His goodness, mercy, and grace.

A Final Blessing

As you close this book, may you be blessed with a renewed heart and strengthened faith. May the stories and lessons from these women inspire you to live fully for God, embracing your unique place in His story.

Walk forward with courage and compassion, knowing that the same God who guided, healed, and empowered these women is with you every step of the way.

May you find comfort in the challenges, strength in the trials, and joy in the victories. And may the lives of these women continue to speak to you, encouraging you to grow closer to the God who loves you deeply and who calls you His own.

Go forth with confidence and faith, knowing that you are a part of something eternal.

In Christ
Rev Minton Thomas